FINDING GOD

This Book
was made possible through the
caring and generosity of
Manny and Rosalyn Rosenthal
of Fort Worth, Texas

FINDING GOD

Ten Jewish Responses

RIFAT SONSINO
DANIEL B. SYME

UNION OF AMERICAN HEBREW CONGREGATIONS

Library of Congress Cataloging-in-Publication Data

Sonsino, Rifat, 1938–
  Finding God.

  Bibliography: p.
  1. God (Judaism)—History of doctrines. I. Syme,
Daniel B. II. Title.
BM610.S58 1986   296.3'11   85-27521
ISBN 0-8074-0312-1

To my Children
Danny and Debbi Sonsino
and
their generation

Rifat Sonsino

To my Parents, Rabbi M. Robert and Sonia Syme
To my Wife, Debbie, and my son, Joshua
To my Brothers, David and Michael ז״ל
and to Dr. Raphael Altman, Dr. Sherwin Lutz
and
Manny Rosenthal
All of whom helped me keep a sacred promise

Daniel B. Syme

Acknowledgments

This volume has benefited from the wisdom and counsel of many individuals. We express our thanks to those rabbis, educators, and lay leaders who read the manuscript in various stages and offered many helpful comments: Rabbis Roland Gittelsohn, Samuel Karff, Bernard Zlotowitz, Howard Laibson, and Emily Feigenson. We extend our gratitude also to Alan Bennett, David Belin, William Hess, Dr. Lenore Sandel, Jan Epstein, Melvin Merians, Gary Metzel, Allan Goldman, Marjorie Rothschild, Joseph Kleiman, Lydia Kukoff, Nina Mizrahi, Deborah Reshotko, and Elaine Zecher.

As always, we express heartfelt appreciation to Aron Hirt-Manheimer, Stuart Benick, Steven Schnur, Josette Knight, and Annette Abramson of the UAHC Department of Publications. They took the raw manuscript and transformed it into a text with their own special and creative magic.

And, finally, we express our deep gratitude to Eppie Begleiter and Muriel Freedman, who typed this manuscript time and time again, who urged us on, and who believed in us.

Rifat Sonsino
Daniel B. Syme

Photo Credits

Contents

Authors' Note

Because the Hebrew Bible uses the masculine form, Bible
translators and many writers refer to God as
"He."
In the text of this book, except in direct quotations, we have
remained true to our conviction, shared by many thinkers, that
God is beyond gender, neither male nor female.

GENERAL INTRODUCTION

This is a book about God. More specifically, it is a book about ways in which Jews have spoken of God through 4,000 years of Jewish history. This book will not attempt to tell you what to believe as a Jew. Rather, it will present a spectrum of theological options that have been explored and affirmed by great Jewish thinkers, ancient and modern.

Today there are large numbers of Jews who avoid speaking about God altogether. Unable to accept the notions that have been presented to them as authoritative, they read themselves out of their religion in a theological sense. This is tragic for two reasons. First, everyone needs to believe in something. Seemingly denied a place in the context of their own religious community, literally tens of thousands of men, women, and young people have turned to other faiths, cults, or exotic groups that offer the possibility of spiritual expression more in keeping with their personal God concept.

Second, such a search is often precipitated by the erroneous notion that their theology is invalid in Jewish terms. Thus, Judaism often loses spiritual adherents as a result of a failure to communicate options for belief that are part and parcel of its history.

In the pages that follow, you will encounter ten distinct

Jewish theological perspectives. In cases where a particular Jewish thinker is closely identified with a system, biographical material about that individual is included. Each of the theologians or philosophers selected here grappled thoughtfully with the mysteries of the universe, and each one has something to say to us about our own lives, as people and as Jews, in response to some or all of the following questions:

- *What is God's nature?* Is God a spirit, a person, a force, or a human invention?
- *Is there one God, or more than one?* Are there divine powers besides God? Do angels exist? Does Satan exist?
- *What is God's name?*
- *How can we know God?* Can we have a personal knowledge of God? Or is God totally beyond human understanding?
- *What is God's relationship to the world?* Did God create the world? Does God intervene in the world? Or is God distant from the world? Can God perform miracles?
- *Does God have a special relationship with the Jewish people?* What is the nature of "the covenant"? What does it mean when Jews speak of "the chosen people"? Are we really "chosen," and, if so, for what?
- *What does God "want" from us?* Are we commanded to "obey" God through the performance of certain acts? Has God "commanded" ritual observances and laws? Or is the idea of commandments, *mitzvot,* a human invention?
- *How does God relate to me?* Does God hear my prayers? Can God help me when I am in trouble or grieving? How can I know if God is listening to me? Is it solely my responsibility to deal with life and its challenges?
- *Why is there evil in the world?* Why do good people suffer and bad people prosper? If God is all-powerful, why do babies die and natural disasters kill so many innocent people? How could God have "let" the Holocaust happen? If God is not all-powerful, why believe in God?

This book will not provide definitive answers to these questions. Rather, it will present ways in which sensitive thinkers have responded to at least some of them, each in his own way. While the theological options presented are by no means exhaustive, we believe that you may recognize yourself and your ideas in the words of these thinkers and thus discover a Jewish theological "role model" for yourself.

You may not have known that such spiritual stances were important components of the Jewish historical experience. That's because most Jews tend not to talk about God. Accordingly, the great majority of Jews receive the implicit message that "the" Jewish God idea is the theology known as "theism," which you will read about in chapter 1, "God in the Bible," and in chapter 2, "God in Rabbinic Literature."

The fact is, there is more, much more. That is why we wrote this book, which is in essence an introduction to Jewish faith options. If we make it possible for one Jew to reclaim his or her Jewish spiritual identity, if we help others to begin to talk about God without ambivalence or embarrassment, if we serve as a catalyst for further study of these and other Jewish thinkers, we will consider our work worthwhile.

1

GOD IN THE BIBLE

Background

The peoples of the ancient Near East accepted without question the existence of divine beings. They did not ask: "Does God exist?" They already knew the answer. What they wanted to know most was: "Who is our God?" "What does our God expect of us?" and, in particular, "What is our God's name?"

Nowhere either in the Pentateuch (the Five Books of Moses) or in the other books of the Hebrew Bible (Prophets and Writings), do we find a passage attempting to prove that God exists. God's existence was never questioned. In fact, according to biblical teaching:

> "The fool says in his heart,
> There is no God."*
> (Pss. 14:1, 53:2)

When God "spoke" with Moses through the Burning Bush, the main concern of Moses was to know God's particular name. We read:

Moses said to God, "When I come to the Israelites and

*Based on the 1917 Standard Jewish Version (SJV), published by the Jewish Publication Society (JPS), Philadelphia.

say to them, 'The God of your fathers has sent me to you,' and they ask me, 'What is His name?' what shall I say to them?" And God said . . . to Moses . . . "Thus shall you speak to the Israelites: The Lord [YHVH], the God of your fathers, the God of Abraham, the God of Isaac, and the God of Jacob, has sent me to you. . . ."*

(Exod. 3:13–15)

The biblical Israelites primarily asked: ". . . Is the Lord present among us or not?" (Exod. 17:7)

They wanted to know if God was "distant," or if they could rely on the power of God to save them from their enemies and provide for their needs in this world.

*Unless otherwise indicated all Bible excerpts will follow the New Jewish Version translation, published by JPS.

Developing an Idea of God

In biblical times, ideas about God changed from period to period and as the Israelites moved from one place to another.

Early in the Bible, we see that most Israelites recognized God as the sole Protector of Israel without, however, denying the existence of other deities. Thus, for example, the superiority of the Israelite God over others is celebrated in the familiar liturgical passage, *Mi Chamochah:*

> Who is like You, Eternal One, among the gods that are worshiped?
> Who is like You, majestic in holiness, awesome in splendor, doing wonders?*
>
> (Exod. 15:11)

The Israelites even regarded certain natural forces as worthy of worship by other nations.

> And when you look up to the sky and behold the sun and the moon and the stars, the whole heavenly host, you must not be lured into bowing down to them or serving them. These the Lord your God allotted to the other peoples [as divinities] everywhere under heaven; but you the Lord took . . . to be His very own people. . . .
>
> (Deut. 4:19–20)

Scholars today recognize that the religion of the Canaanites, the local people in ancient Israel, had a strong influence on the biblical views of God. The Israelites "borrowed" a number of ideas from these Canaanites. Thus, for example, Israel's God was viewed not only as the Creator of the universe (see Gen.

*Quoted from *Gates of Prayer,* published by the Central Conference of American Rabbis, 1975.

1 and 2) but also, like Baal, the Canaanite fertility god, as a powerful Deity "riding upon the clouds" (Ps. 68:5) and a Provider of grain, wine, and oil (Hos. 2:10; Ps. 65:10–14).

In time, the belief in the existence of gods for other peoples faded away, and the ancient Israelites decided that even what others considered divine beings were nothing but idols. For instance, one great prophet, usually referred to as the Second Isaiah (about the sixth century B.C.E.), said that other gods do not exist at all.

> Why, you are less than nothing,
> Your effect is less than nullity;
> One who chooses you is an abomination.
>
> (Isa. 41:24)

And the same statement of faith is also found in the Book of Psalms:

> All the gods of the peoples are mere idols,
> but the Lord made the heavens.
>
> (Ps. 96:5)

A Composite View of God

What did the biblical Jew think of God? We must begin by stating that the Bible does not contain a single and systematic notion of God. Ideas about God, sometimes very different from one another, are spread throughout Scriptures. What the Israelites thought of God changed and developed in the course of time. Therefore, no particular source or author can be taken as "the" biblical view of God. It is possible, however, to identify a few major beliefs which the final editors of the Bible would most likely have recognized and accepted as valid. This composite view of the "biblical Israelites" represents a culmination of various stages which began about 1800 B.C.E. and ended with the final version or "redaction" of the Bible which took place about the last third of the first century C.E.

Following are the major components of the biblical view.

1. Monotheism: There Is Only One God

For the biblical Israelite, God was One, the only One. There were no other gods. As Deut. 6:4 expresses it: "Hear, O Israel! The Lord is our God, the Lord alone."

To be sure, the Bible often refers to "angels" (e.g., Pss. 103:20; 148:2), "divine beings" (e.g., Pss. 29:1; 89:7), "the host of heaven" (e.g., 1 Kings 22:19), and other heavenly creatures. These, however, in no way compromise God's uniqueness. All of them are only messengers, doing the bidding of the one and only God. In contrast to the gods of the ancient Near East, Israel's God does not belong to a divine group, either as its member or as its leader. Also, unlike other gods, the biblical God does not have a female counterpart. God does not have a wife, a father, a mother, a son, or a daughter. God stands alone.

2. God Has a Name

In the Bible, God is often referred to as *El* or *Elohim* (God), *El Shaddai* (Almighty), *Adon* (Lord), *Tzur* (Rock), *Av* (Father), *Melech* (King). All of these names were used to help the people relate to the ways in which God touched their lives. Similarly, a friend's proper name might be Sarah, but you might also refer to her as "my friend," "my confidante," or "my cousin."

In the Bible, God also has a proper name, YHVH, *Yahveh,* the Lord. In reality, we do not know how to pronounce this name, because in ancient times Hebrew did not use vowels and the Bible provides no clues as to its proper pronunciation. Look at the letters DBRH. Without vowels, you might pronounce it "Dibroh" or "Dobreh." Only after you knew the missing vowels could you determine the correct pronunciation, "Deborah." Though the biblical Israelites must have known their God's name, fearing that this name might be misused, or that saying God's real name might bring some punishment, a group of scribes of the sixth-seventh century C.E., called the Masoretes, decided that God's proper name should be read as *Adonai* (my Lord), even though this pronunciation has no relationship whatsoever to the consonants YHVH. To this day, some Jews write G-d, a practice whose roots can be traced to the biblical period.

The meaning of YHVH is not clear. It seems to come from a verb in Hebrew which means "existence." According to the Torah, the personal name of God was "announced" for the first time by Moses.

> I appeared to Abraham, Isaac, and Jacob as *El Shaddai* [God Almighty], but I did not make Myself known to them by My name יהוה [YHVH—the Lord].
>
> (Exod. 6:3)

The name YHVH seems to have been known by others prior to Moses. For example, by the people before the Flood (Gen. 4:26), by Abraham (Gen. 14:22), by Laban (Gen. 24:31), by Jacob (Gen. 28:13). Through this verse in Exodus, then, the editors of the Bible seem to be stressing that Moses was not introducing a new God to the Israelites. The God who spoke to Moses was the same God who led the patriarchs in their wanderings, but was now reappearing in a more dramatic way in order to translate into reality the promises addressed to the ancestors of Israel.

3. No One Knows What God Looks Like

The Bible instructs the Israelites not to represent God by a sculptured image, not to make idols, as did other peoples of ancient times.

> You shall not make for yourself a sculptured image [of God]. . . . You shall not bow down to them or serve them. . . .
>
> (Exod. 20:4–5)

The question that comes to mind here is how the Israelites imagined God. Did they consider God as having a particular form? Did they attempt to describe God?

In a remarkable passage in Exod. 24:11, we read that Moses and a few elders of Israel "beheld God, and they ate and drank." The text, however, does not say what these people actually saw. Most likely, the narrative refers not to the Deity but to the platform on which they believed God "stood."

> . . . Under His feet there was the likeness of a pavement of sapphire, like the very sky for purity.
>
> (Exod. 24:10)

Even Moses, who "knew" God "face to face" (Deut. 34:10), was, according to the Torah, allowed to see only "the likeness of the Lord" (Num. 12:8). He was told that "you will see My back; but My face must not be seen" (Exod. 33:23).

Among the prophets, both Micaiah ben Imlah (1 Kings 22:19) and Isaiah (6:1) report having "seen" God, yet neither one provides us with a description of God. Similarly, Ezekiel describes a blurred image of God when he states that "upon this semblance of a throne, there was the semblance of a human form" (1:26; cf. Gen. 1:27). When Elijah the prophet "meets" God in the desert, he proclaims that God was not in the wind, or in the earthquake, or in the fire, but in the "still small voice" (SJV/1 Kings 19:12) of conscience. At Sinai, the people of Israel believed they heard the "voice" of God, but saw no form (Deut. 4:12, 15–18). The message of the biblical text, therefore, seems to be that God is incomparable in majesty and totally different from us. We can feel God's presence, but we cannot see God's likeness.

4. God Acts in the World

According to the Bible, even though we cannot see God or describe God in human terms, we can easily recognize God's presence in the world through the beauty of human nature and God's influence in history.

a. God as the sole Creator of the world:
Jews of the biblical period saw God as the Creator par ex-
cellence. The universe, they believed, came into being
through the creative power of the divine "word." We read
in Psalms:

> For He spoke, and it was;
> He commanded, and it endured.
> > (33:9; see also Gen. 1)

Israel's monotheism rejected any notion of partnership with
other deities in the process of creation. Other peoples of the
ancient Near East believed that there were many gods before
the creation of the world, and that the world came into existence as a result of a conflict among various supreme beings.
For example, in the Babylonian creation story, the earth was
created when a group of younger gods, under the leadership
of Marduk, the god of the city of Babylon, finally defeated the
goddess Tiamat and her divine allies. Marduk split Tiamat in
two, like a "shellfish." With one part he made the sky and with
the other, we are led to believe, the earth.
Israel's God, however, acted alone. At the time of creation,
there was no other deity but God. Once the world was created,
God also established a predictable order for it.

> He made the moon to mark the seasons;
> the sun knows when to set.
> You bring on darkness and it is night. . . .
> > (Ps. 104:19–20)

Also, God's creation is renewed continually.

> He makes clouds rise from the end of the earth;
> He makes lightning for the rain;
> He releases the wind from His vaults.
> > (Ps. 135:7)

We humans were created and placed in an orderly environment. No individual can ever claim possession of the earth.
"The earth is the Lord's and all that it holds, the world and its
inhabitants" (Ps. 24:1). No one is allowed to sell a piece of land
beyond reclaim, "for the land is Mine" (Lev. 25:23). Humanity
acts only as a keeper of a precious gift. Ultimately, all peoples
are "but strangers resident with Me" (Lev. 25:23). They are
temporarily placed here on earth. But "The Lord will reign for
ever and ever" (Exod. 15:18).

b. God in history:

In biblical thinking, God's might and concern for humanity
are revealed through historical events. Thus, for example, the
Exodus from Egypt is viewed not as a human act but as the
work of a powerful God. In the Ten Commandments, we read:
"I the Lord am your God who brought you out of the land of
Egypt" (Exod. 20:2). Similarly, in a very ancient passage, which
is also part of our Passover Haggadah, an Israelite is asked to
recite:

> The Lord freed us from Egypt by a mighty hand. . . .
> He brought us to this place and gave us this land. . . .
> (Deut. 26:8–9)

Israel's God controls the affairs of the Israelites and those
who come in contact with them. Thus, not only did God bring
the Israelites into the Holy Land, but also promised to protect
them from the many nations in Canaan:

> . . . The Hittites, Girgashites, Amorites, Canaanites,
> Perizzites, Hivites, and Jebusites, seven nations much
> larger than you—and the Lord your God delivers
> them to you and you defeat them. . . .
> (Deut. 7:1–2)

At times, the Bible portrays God punishing Israel by using
other agents. Thus, for example, during the reign of Jehu, king

of Israel (ninth century B.C.E.), we read: "In those days the Lord began to reduce Israel; and Hazael [king of Syria] harassed them throughout the territory of Israel" (2 Kings 10:32). It was God who sent "Assyria, rod of My Anger . . . against an ungodly nation" (Isa. 10:5–6), namely, Israel.

It was also God who "commissioned" Cyrus, king of Persia, to liberate Israel from Babylonian captivity. It was this Cyrus who "shall fulfill all My [God's] purposes" (Isa. 44:28).

In short, God acts in the world both in a direct and indirect manner, for the benefit or detriment of Israel, depending upon Israel's adherence to its special covenant with God.

5. God Has a Special Relationship with Israel

According to the Torah, God "chose" the people of Israel out of a multitude of nations.

> . . . You are a people consecrated to the Lord your God: of all the peoples on earth the Lord your God chose you to be His treasured people.
>
> (Deut. 7:6)

Similarly, in the Song of Moses, we read:

> . . . The Lord's portion is His people,
> Jacob His own allotment.
> He found him in a desert region,
> In an empty howling waste.
> He engirded him, watched over him,
> Guarded him as the pupil of His eye.
> (Deut. 32:9–10)

This singling out, or "election," was not based on a special merit of the Israelites.

> It is not because you are the most numerous of peoples that the Lord set His heart on you and chose you

—indeed, you are the smallest of peoples; but it was because the Lord loved you and kept the oath He made to your fathers that the Lord freed you. . . .

(Deut. 7:7–8)

According to Jewish tradition, the Israelites were chosen because of the loyalty of the patriarchs and matriarchs to God. It is this special commitment that constitutes the basis of their election.

Because He loved your fathers, He chose their offspring after them. . . .

(Deut. 4:37)

Israel's chosenness, however, does not give them special privileges. On the contrary, it imposes upon them greater responsibilities. The prophet Amos clearly states:

You alone have I singled out
Of all the families of the earth—
That is why I will call you to account
For all your iniquities.

(Amos 3:2)

Israel's election also implies a particular purpose. Israel is to become a "light to the nations" (Isa. 42:6, 49:6), an agent who transmits the word of God to the peoples of the earth. Ultimately, the election of Israel will be a source of blessing for all: "All the families of the earth shall bless themselves by you" (Gen. 12:3). This means—as one scholar explained it—the nations of the world will point to Abraham as their ideal, either in blessing themselves or one another.

The doctrine of chosenness has been a source of both great pride and pain to the Jewish people over the centuries. Those of other faiths often used this teaching as a pretext for cruel oppression of the Jews. In response, our Sages taught that the

Jews were "chosen" only after every other people on earth rejected that status and that responsibility. One rabbinic legend even asserts that the Israelites accepted their role only after God lifted Mount Sinai over their heads and threatened to destroy the people if they did not embrace their mission.

These teachings did not deter the haters, but the doctrine did unify the Jews, gave them a special sense of destiny, and served as a bond, a link to the past and to the future as well. Just as each of us acts in a special way when we feel special, so the Jewish people, conscious of their uniqueness, performed deeds and embraced values that have transformed human history.

6. Israel Has a Covenant with God

A covenant is primarily a contract which binds all those who take part in it. In the Bible, God extended covenants to individuals, such as Noah (Gen. 9), Abraham (Gen. 15 and 17), and David (2 Sam. 7). But, on Mount Sinai (also called Mt. Horeb), God entered into a special covenant, a *berit,* with the entire people of Israel. This covenant was made not only with the desert generation but also with the generations of the Israelites yet to come, including us.

> I make this covenant, with its sanctions, not with you alone, but both with those who are standing here with us this day before the Lord our God and with those who are not with us here this day.
>
> (Deut. 29:13–14)

This covenant at Sinai, which in time became the foundation of Jewish religious life, imposes duties and obligations on both parties. God promises to protect Israel, and Israel swears to be loyal and true to the conditions of the covenant.

Over and over again, the biblical text reminds the Israelites of their responsibilities as well as of God's promises:

Now, if you obey the Lord your God, to observe faithfully all His commandments . . . the Lord your God will set you high above all the nations of the earth.

(Deut. 28:1)

When the Israelites failed to carry out their part of the covenant, the Bible relates:

". . . They have returned to the iniquities of their fathers of old. . . . They, too, have followed other gods and served them. The House of Israel and the House of Judah have broken the covenant which I made with their fathers."

Assuredly, thus said the Lord: I am going to bring upon them disaster. . . .

(Jer. 11:10–11)

The biblical God, however, is also a God of compassion. We are assured that the temporary backsliding of Israel will not cause a permanent breaking of the bond which was so lovingly established in the past. There will come a time, God proclaims, when the obligations of the *berit* will not be imposed from the outside, but will be inscribed in the heart of every Israelite. Carrying out the laws of the covenant will become second nature to every individual.

See, a time is coming—declares the Lord—when I will make a new covenant with the House of Israel and the House of Judah. . . . I will put My Teaching into their inmost being and inscribe it upon their hearts. Then I will be their God, and they shall be My people.

(Jer. 31:31, 33)

7. God Requires Ethical Behavior

The biblical God of Israel is a source of ethical values. Rituals alone are not enough. More than anything else, God requires good behavior.

> For I desire goodness, not sacrifice;
> Obedience to God, rather than burnt offerings.
>
> (Hos. 6:6)

Just as I am "holy," so you be "holy" declares God (Lev. 19:2). The prophet Micah clearly states God's primary requirements:

> "He has told you, O man, what is good,
> And what the Lord requires of you:
> Only to do justice
> And to love goodness,
> And to walk modestly with your God. . . ."
>
> (Mic. 6:8)

8. God Is a Personal God

The biblical God was also portrayed as a personal God, to whom a number of human traits were ascribed. The Israelites already assumed that God was not made of flesh and blood. "I am God, not man" (Hos. 11:9). Yet, at the same time, they believed that God embodied all the highest human qualities. This made God *both* a faraway supreme power and an approachable and caring deity.

For example, like a parent, God lovingly watches over us.

> As a father has compassion for his children,
> so the Lord has compassion for those who fear [meaning "revere"] Him.
>
> (Ps. 103:13)

At times, we are told, God becomes "jealous" (or zealous) of divine sovereignty (Exod. 20:5, 34:14). Or, God may display "anger" at the people of Israel (Num. 11:33). Yet, God's "steadfast love" *(chesed)* towards them endures forever (Hos. 2:21; Ps. 100:5).

God is "a compassionate and gracious God, slow to anger, abounding in kindness, renouncing punishment" (Jon. 4:2).

An Israelite in trouble can approach God with words of supplication, with assurance that personal needs will be met.

> The Lord is near to all who call Him,
> to all who call Him with sincerity.
> (Ps. 145:18)

9. We Cannot Understand Why the Righteous Suffer

One of the major assumptions in the Bible is that God punishes the wicked and rewards the righteous.

> The righteous can look forward to joy,
> But the hope of the wicked is doomed.
> (Prov. 10:28)

> I have been young and am now old,
> but I have never seen a righteous man abandoned,
> or his children seeking bread.
> (Ps. 37:25)

Yet, along with others in the ancient Near East, the biblical Israelites at times complained that this was not always the case. The wicked are not always punished, nor are the righteous always rewarded. On many occasions the innocent do suffer for the sins of others. The question is asked: How can a good God allow this to happen? We find many examples of this outcry in the Bible.

Abraham:

> Far be it from You to do such a thing, to bring death
> upon the innocent as well as the guilty, so that inno-
> cent and guilty fare alike. Far be it from You! Shall not
> the Judge of all the earth deal justly?
>
> (Gen. 18:25)

The prophet Jeremiah:

> . . . Why does the way of the wicked prosper? . . .
>
> (Jer. 12:1)

The prophet Habakkuk:

> You whose eyes are too pure to look upon evil,
> Who cannot countenance wrongdoing,
> Why do You countenance treachery,
> And stand by idle
> While the one in the wrong devours
> The one in the right?
>
> (Hab. 1:13)

The Psalmist:

> . . . I saw the wicked at ease.
>
> (Ps. 73:3)

The answers to this difficult question are not uniform in the
biblical writings. Various attempts were made to deal with it.
Some, as Eliphaz, maintained that suffering is the deserved
punishment for sin.

> As I have seen, those who plow evil
> And sow mischief reap them.
>
> (Job 4:8)

Others have argued that suffering is only a test.

> Remember the long way that the Lord your God has
> made you travel in the wilderness these past forty
> years, that He might test you by hardships to learn
> what was in your hearts: Whether you would keep His
> commandments or not.
>
> (Deut. 8:2)

There were those who gave up the question and agreed that
evil is haphazard and morally meaningless. It touches every
one of us, whether we are good or not.

> That is the sad thing about all that goes on under the
> sun: that the same fate is in store for all. . . .
>
> (Eccl. 9:3)

There were some, as Isaiah and Zophar, who thought that
the question of the suffering of the innocent is beyond our
comprehension. God cannot be judged by human yardsticks.

> As the heavens are high above the earth,
> So are My ways high above your ways. . . .
>
> (Isa. 55:9)

> Would you discover the mystery of God?
> Would you discover the limit of the Almighty?
>
> (Job. 11:7)

In spite of this uncertainty, the biblical Israelite was urged
to return to God for strength and support and perhaps a new
insight, as the Psalmist did under similar circumstances:

> I applied myself to understand this,
> but it seemed a hopeless task

till I entered God's Sanctuary
and reflected on their fate.
                    (Ps. 73:16–17)

In Summary

There are many points of contact between the Bible and the ancient Near Eastern texts about God. Israel's biblical God incorporates a number of characteristics attributed to various other gods, but Israel's God surpasses them. Rather than being part of a divine assembly, Israel's God acts alone. Rejecting the custom prevalent among other nations, the Bible prohibits the making of sculptured images of God. The gods of other nations acted within the cycle of nature and often were indistinguishable from them. There were separate gods for weather, rain, sun, moon, etc. In Israel, God stands outside of this cycle and is not identified with it. "It is I, the Lord, who made everything," declares Isaiah (44:24) on behalf of God. Israel's God puts a heavy emphasis on ethical behavior. God has established a special covenant with Israel and, yet, is also the only savior of humanity, "Turn to Me and gain success, / All the ends of earth! . . ." (Isa. 45:22)

2

GOD IN RABBINIC

LITERATURE

Background

Jews historically have studied the Torah as a guide to how we should conduct our lives. At times, however, biblical directives seemed unclear or incomplete, prompting the people to turn to their teachers, the Rabbis, for explanation and clarification of the text. At first, these interpretations were preserved as an oral tradition, passed on from one generation to the next. Eventually, they were committed to writing, a process scholars believe began as early as the first century C.E. Perhaps the Rabbis' intention was to help their students learn the material with greater ease. It is also probable that the Sages did so out of fear that, if these teachings were kept in the oral stage, an entire body of literature might be lost forever. Whatever their motives, their teachings were collected into various forms of "rabbinic literature."

The Scope of the Literature

We can divide the large body of early rabbinic writings into three major types:

1. *Collections of laws:* Among these, the foremost was the *Mishnah,* edited by Rabbi Judah Hanasi in the early part of the third century C.E. The *Mishnah* was then supplemented by further commentaries in Aramaic, called *Gemara.* The *Gemara* together with the text of the *Mishnah* made up the Talmud, which appeared in two different versions: the Jerusalem Talmud (about 400 C.E.) and the Babylonian Talmud (about 500 C.E.).

2. *Midrash Halachah:* These are basically legal commentaries on the laws of the Pentateuch. The most prominent are: *Mekilta* (on the Book of Exodus, from chapter 12 to 23:19), *Sifra* (on the Book of Leviticus), and *Sifre* (on the books of Numbers and Deuteronomy, chapters 12–26).

3. *Midrash Aggadah:* These are mostly sermonic materials written for purposes of religious and moral edification, for example, *Bereshit Rabbah* (on the Book of Genesis), *Pirke Avot* (Sayings of the Fathers, part of the *Mishnah*), *Seder Olam* (a historical record of events from the creation of the world to Alexander the Great and beyond).

No Systematic Doctrine

Throughout this vast literature, we find many rabbinic statements about God. Yet, rabbinic thought on this subject is not organized in a systematic way. There is no one rabbinic book which deals exclusively with questions of theology. Therefore, in order to understand what the Rabbis believed and taught about God, it is necessary to comb the texts for appropriate illustrative material.

The sayings of the Rabbis on theological matters were not dogmatic and did not carry the same weight as their legal decisions which were binding. Indeed, in the rabbinic literature, it is possible to find sharply contradictory teachings on faith without any attempt on the part of the writers to resolve their differences. In spite of this diversity, however, there seems to be a broad consensus on what God meant to the Rabbis.

1. God Exists

Though the Rabbis took the existence of God for granted, we begin to see in the rabbinic literature attempts to "prove" the existence of a universal God. According to one midrash, an unbeliever came to see Rabbi Akiba and asked him: "Who created the world?" Rabbi Akiba said: "Who made the garment which you are wearing?" The other replied: "Obviously a weaver!" "Prove it to me," said Rabbi Akiba. "What proof can I show you? Don't you know that a weaver makes clothes?" "And don't you know," Rabbi Akiba answered, "that God is the Creator of the universe?" When Rabbi Akiba's students asked that he explain his reasoning better, he said: "Just as a house implies that a builder built it, so the world makes known God as the one who created it."

According to the Rabbis, what others called "gods" were merely idols. Thus, for example, in explaining the second of the Ten Commandments, "You shall have no other gods beside Me" (Exod. 20:3), they said:

"Other gods." [These were the words upon which they were commenting.]

But are they gods? Has it not been said: "And have cast their gods into the fire; for they were no gods" [SJV/Isa. 37:19]?

What then does Scripture mean when it says: "Other gods"?

Merely those which others called gods.

(*Mekilta, Bachodesh* VI, vol. 2, p. 239; JPS, 1933)

2. There Is Only One God

The belief in one God remained basic with the Rabbis. As in the Bible, they, too, taught that God is the only God.

An earthly king . . . has dukes and viceroys, who share with him in the burden of rule, and also have a share in the honor with which he is honored, but God is not so; He has no duke or governor and no lieutenant. No other with Him does His work, but He does it alone. No other bears the burden with Him, but He bears it alone. Therefore He alone is to be praised.*

(Midrash on Psalms 149:1)

The Rabbis introduced many new terms for God: *Hagevurah* (The Mighty One), *Harachaman* (The Merciful One), *Hakadosh baruch Hu* (The Holy One, blessed is He), *Shamayim* (Heavens), *Hamakom* (The Place), *Ribono shel olam* (Master of the universe), *Mi she-amar vehayah ha-olam* (He who spoke and the world came into being), *Avinu shebashamayim* (our Father in heaven), and many others. These were created as substitutes for the proper name of God. They were to be used in order not to take the real name of God in vain.

For the Rabbis, as in the Bible, the fact that God is referred to by various names does not mean that there are many gods.

*Quoted in *A Rabbinic Anthology,* Montefiore and Loewe, no. 20, p. 11; Meridian Books, 1963.

When I am judging created things, I am called "God," and, when I am waging war against the wicked, I am called "Lord of Hosts." When I suspend judgment for a man's sins, I am called *El Shaddai* [Almighty God], and, when I am merciful towards My world, I am called *"Adonai,"* for *"Adonai"* refers to the Attribute of Mercy, as it is said [SJV/Exod. 34:6], "The Lord, the Lord [*Adonai, Adonai*], God, merciful and gracious."

(Exodus Rabbah, Shemot III, 6; Soncino)

If the Rabbis had any major concern, it was with those who claimed that not one but *two* different gods operated in the world, one in charge of good and one in charge of evil. Thus, for example, they taught:

[Scripture] would not let the nations of the world have an excuse for saying that there are two powers but declares: "I am the Lord your God. I am He who was in Egypt and I am He who was at the sea. I am He who was at Sinai. I am He who was in the past and I am He who will be in the future."

(Mekilta, Bachodesh IV, vol. 2, p. 231)

3. Angels Are God's Messengers

In the opinion of the Rabbis, much of God's work is often performed by messengers, the angels. We saw that in the Bible God was portrayed as surrounded by a heavenly host, ready to obey their Master. (See chapter 1, p. 9.) In rabbinic literature, too, we find that angels are poised to serve God in a multitude of ways. These angels are God's celestial soldiers. They walk upright and are endowed with understanding. They are viewed as spirits, winds, fire, etc. They can fly in the air and move from one end of the world to another. Though created by God, they do not eat or drink. They do not give birth to other angels and they do not die. They can only be destroyed by God.

A number of angels appear in rabbinic texts. These angels function in every conceivable way. Some regulate the movements of the heavenly bodies. Others control the seas. Some angels act as guardians of individuals or nations. There are angels who act as court scribes. Others accompany people on Friday nights as they go from the synagogue to their homes. They act as advocates before the heavenly court. They save individuals from danger, visit the sick, and perform a host of other divinely ordained tasks. Often, these heavenly beings have names, such as Gabriel, Michael, and Raphael. At times, angels are called to perform specific functions. For example, Gabriel is the angel of revelation (already in the Bible; see Daniel 8:16, 9:21), while Michael champions the cause of Israel. And Samael, the Angel of Death, takes people from the world at the appointed time.

Though the Rabbis frequently talked about angels, they took great care to assure that the angels would never be confused with God. Portraying them in any art form was strictly forbidden, and making them objects of veneration was heresy. The angels were considered only servants of God, pure and simple.

Their role was also clearly limited: Though they sometimes communicated God's message to individuals, the angels were not mediators and they did not convey the prayers of human beings to God. Jews prayed directly to God. The Rabbis, who believed that God is the only One worthy of worship, would hardly have allowed prayers to be directed to angels or transmitted by them.

> If a man is in distress, let him not call on Michael or Gabriel, but let him call direct on Me, and I will hearken to him straightaway.*
> (Jerusalem Talmud, *Berachot* 9, no. 1, f. 13a, l. 69)

*Quoted in *A Rabbinic Anthology*, no. 48, p. 23.

4. God Judges the World

Though consistent in their belief in God's unity, the Rabbis taught that God's "personality" included two different aspects: mercy *(middat harachamim)* and justice *(middat hadin)*. When God shows mercy, the name *Adonai* is employed, whereas *Elohim* corresponds to God's justice. The various names of God, then, are used as literary clues to alert us to God's stance vis-à-vis the world at that moment.

Through justice, God gives assurance to humanity that nothing will happen by chance and that the wicked will get the punishment they deserve. Through mercy, however, God considers individual cases and tempers harsh decrees. The world cannot exist without both:

> If I create the world on the basis of mercy alone, its sins will be great; [if I create it] on the basis of judgment alone, the world cannot exist. Hence, I will create it on the basis of judgment and of mercy, and may it then stand!
>
> *(Genesis Rabbah, Bereshit* XII, 15; Soncino)

Of the two, God's mercy is considered more important:

> Which attribute is greater: the attribute of goodness or the attribute of punishment? The attribute of goodness.
>
> *(Sifre Numbers, Naso* 8)

The Rabbis even put a special prayer in the mouth of God:

> May it be My will that My mercy may suppress My anger, and that My mercy may prevail over My (other) attributes [of justice and judgment] so that I may deal with My children in the attribute of mercy, and, on their behalf, stop short of the limit of strict justice.
>
> *(Berachot* 7a; Soncino)

It is interesting to note that the text of both the Bible and rabbinic literature often ascribes human emotions to God. When Israel experienced great suffering, or when Jews enjoyed great prosperity, it was not uncommon to find those events portrayed as a result of God's "feeling anger" or "being pleased." God is thus presented as "anthropopathic" (anthropo = human; pathic = emotional).

The words "anthropopathic" and "anthropomorphic" (having a body) are important words for our theological vocabulary, as are the words "omnipotent" (all powerful) and "omniscient" (all knowing). Many faiths and many thinkers, Judaism and Jews among them, found our human vocabulary too limited to describe God. Therefore, they used the words available to them to try to convey their sense of God. Did the Rabbis really believe that God "got angry" or "was pleased" with the Jews? We don't know for certain, but it is probable that they did the best they could to speak about God in the language of the people whom they taught. In fact, the Rabbis said: "The Torah speaks in human language."

5. God and Israel Are Joined by a Special Bond

The Rabbis talked lovingly about an intimate relationship between God and Israel. God, for the Rabbis, is Israel's parent, protector, and savior. The love that unites the two is unbreakable.

> For even if all the idolaters were to assemble to quench the love between God and Israel they would be powerless.
>
> (*Exodus Rabbah, Vayakhel* XLIX, 1)

Similarly, we find:

> God said to Israel: You have made Me the only object of your love in the world . . . so I shall make you the only object of My love in the world.
>
> (*Berachot* 6a)

The relationship of love is mutual. Just as God loves Israel, so does Israel love and worship God.

> My beloved is mine and I am his [The Song of Songs 2:16]. [Israel says:] He is my God, and I am His people; . . . He is my Father, . . . and I am His son . . .; He is my Shepherd, . . . and I am His flock . . .; He is my Guardian, . . . and I am His vineyard.
> (*The Song of Songs Rabbah* II, 16; Soncino)

In rabbinic thinking, Israel was chosen by God from among all the nations of the earth. As one rabbinic prayer expressed it:

> In love and favor, O God, You have chosen us from all the peoples, exalting us by hallowing us with Your *mitzvot.*
> (*Gates of Prayer,* p. 482)

The reason for this chosenness, however, was debated among the Sages. For some Rabbis, Israel's election was predestined before the creation of the world. Others maintained that the Israelites were chosen because they recognized God as their ruler when they crossed the Red Sea. Still others argued it was because of their humility that God chose them.

It is a basic tenet of rabbinic literature, undoubtedly developed in order to establish the authority of rabbinic legal explanations, that God revealed, not only a Written Torah *(Torah shebichetav)* at Mount Sinai, but also an Oral Torah *(Torah shebe-alpeh)* equally binding, which explains and supplements the Written Law. The giving of both the Written and Oral Torah to the people of Israel was an act of love. For, we are told, God first made the rounds among all the other nations, offering the Torah to them. But they refused to accept it on God's terms.

But when He came to the Israelites . . . they all opened
their mouths and said [SJV/Exod. 24:7]: "All that the
Lord has said, will we do, and obey."

(*Mekilta, Bachodesh* V, vol. 2, p. 235)

The Torah imposes responsibilities upon the Israelites, but
it also helps them to become better human beings. Every individual, the Rabbis taught, operates with two inclinations: the
inclination to do good *(yetzer hatov)* and the inclination to do
evil *(yetzer hara)*. The goal, however, is for every person to
overcome the inclination to do evil and behave in such a way
so as to bring blessing to others.

So God says to the Israelites . . . "I created within you
the inclination to do evil [*yetzer hara*], but I created
the Torah with which to season it. As long as you
occupy yourselves with the Torah, the *yetzer* will not
rule over you."

(*Sifre Deuteronomy, Ekev* 45)

6. God Is a Personal God

According to the Rabbis, we cannot see or understand the
greatness of God because our knowledge is limited. As the
Talmud puts it:

The emperor said to Rabbi Joshua b. Hananiah: "I
wish to see your God." He replied: "You cannot see
Him." "Indeed," said the emperor, "I will see Him."
He went and placed the emperor facing the sun during the summer solstice and said to him, "Look up at
it." He replied, "I cannot." Said Rabbi Joshua, "If at
the sun which is but one of the ministers that attend
the Holy One, blessed be He, you cannot look, how
then can you presume to look upon the Divine Presence!"

(*Chullin* 59b, 60a; Soncino)

Yet God's majesty does not mean that God is distant and aloof. The Rabbis stressed that God is approachable. Even though the heavens are God's primary residence (as the expression, *Avinu shebashamayim,* "Our Father in heaven," seems to imply), God is as near as the ground upon which we walk.

> A heathen once asked R. Joshua b. Korha: Why did God choose a thorn bush from which to speak to Moses? . . . [God spoke from the thorn bush] To teach you that no place is devoid of God's presence, not even a thorn bush.
>
> (*Exodus Rabbah, Shemot* II, 5)

Commenting on the biblical statement, "Behold, I will stand before you upon the rock in Horeb" (Exod. 17:6), one rabbi taught:

> God said to him [Moses], "Wherever you find a mark of men's feet, there I am before you."
>
> (*Mekilta, Vayassa* VII, vol. 2, p. 133)

God is near to every individual who calls in sincerity.

> A man enters a synagogue, and stands behind a pillar, and prays in a whisper, and God hears his prayer, and so it is with all His creatures. Can there be a nearer God than this? He is as near to His creatures as the ear to the mouth.*
>
> (Jerusalem Talmud, *Berachot* 9, no. 1, f. 13a, l.17)

God cares about people and looks after their needs. A rabbi, pointing to many biblical texts in which God is portrayed as doing deeds of kindness, says:

*Quoted in *A Rabbinic Anthology,* no. 46, p. 22.

> We find that the Holy One, blessed be He, blesses
> bridegrooms, adorns brides, visits the sick, buries the
> dead, and recites the blessing for mourners.
> *(Genesis Rabbah, Bereshit* VIII, 13)

People must follow the example of God.

> As He clothed the naked, . . . visited the sick, . . .
> comforted the mourners, buried the dead, . . . so
> should you.
> *(Sotah* 14a)

For the Rabbis, the nearness of God is determined by our
conduct. We can bring God closer to us or we can keep God
far away. How so?

> When a person is mean and does things which are not
> correct, his actions remove him from the *Shechinah*
> (Divine Presence), as it is said: "Your sins have sepa-
> rated between you and your God" [SJV/Isa. 59:2]. But
> when a person does good deeds and pursues Torah
> studies, his actions bring him closer to the *Shechinah.*
> *(Seder Eliahu Rabba,* Friedmann, p. 104;
> Jerusalem, 1960)

The Rabbis believed that God is totally different from people. Yet, by picturing God as a near—or immanent—God who
takes personal interest in the affairs of humanity, they human-
ized God and made the Holy One approachable by any individual.

7. On the Suffering of the Righteous
The fact that righteous people suffer challenged the imagination of the Rabbis. Though they did not deal with the theological aspects of this mystery, the early Rabbis discussed more
pragmatic questions as to how a person should respond to

yissurin, loosely translated as suffering or chastisement.

The Rabbis accepted *yissurin* as part of the human condition. Sometimes it is possible to find the reason behind it; often it is not. One of the main rabbinic assumptions is that suffering frequently comes because of sin.

> Raba [some say, R. Hisda] says: If a man sees that painful sufferings visit him, let him examine his conduct. . . . If he examines and finds nothing [objectionable], let him attribute it to the neglect of the study of the Torah. . . . If he did attribute it [thus], and still did not find [this to be the cause], let him be sure that these are chastenings of love. . . .
>
> *(Berachot* 5a)

A much more important question for the Rabbis was how to respond to *yissurin.* The general attitude of the Rabbis was that one should accept it. For, not only does suffering purify the soul, but it can even bring salvation to the world.

> Rabbi Joshua b. Levi said: He who accepts gladly the sufferings of this world brings salvation to the world.
>
> *(Ta-anit* 8a)

The Rabbis seem to have recognized that suffering may have a purpose, though it is beyond human understanding to determine its role within the divine plan for the universe. Rabbi Yannai's statement can be taken as a clear expression of this approach.

> It is not in our power to [understand] the prosperity of the wicked, nor the *yissurin* of the righteous.
>
> (Avot 4:19)

8. There Is an Afterlife and Bodily Resurrection

According to the Rabbis, this world is not the only one. There is another world called *ha-olam haba* (the world-to-come). This expression is used in rabbinic literature in relation to two consecutive periods in the life of humanity. First, *ha-olam haba* includes a vision of a time when the Messiah will come, when righteousness and peace will be established for all, and Israel will be secured in its own land.

The word "messiah" in Hebrew means "anointed one." Who was anointed? Primarily, the kings of Israel. It is particularly important to recognize that the Rabbis used the word "messiah" in a very specific way. The Jewish people had loved King David. David's son, Solomon, built the Temple in Jerusalem and preserved peace for all Israel. Unfortunately, after Solomon's death, Jeroboam, the son of Nebat, led a rebellion against Rehoboam, the son of Solomon.

The civil war resulted in a split in the Jewish people. Jeroboam became king of ten of the twelve tribes of Israel, while Rehoboam ruled over the remaining two. Some time later, in 721 B.C.E., the Assyrians defeated Jeroboam's kingdom in war and carried the Jews into exile, where they disappeared. They became known as "The Ten Lost Tribes of Israel."

From that moment on, a dream was born in the heart of every Jew. The dream was that one day another descendant of the beloved King David, another "anointed one," would reassume the throne of a reunited kingdom and restore the greatness, peace, and tranquility of an earlier age.

As centuries passed, it became clear that the dream would not be realized. Yet, the idea had become so much a part of Jewish identity that it endured as a sort of spiritual ideal.

The followers of Jesus tried to claim—and assert today—that Jesus was a descendant of King David and the Messiah for whom the Jews had waited for so long. We Jews respect the beliefs of others. Yet, we realize that:

a. Jesus did not reunite Israel.

b. Jesus did not bring peace and righteousness to the entire world. Therefore, we do not recognize Jesus as the Messiah, just as we do not accept the divinity of *any* mortal being.

There was also a second aspect to the rabbinic idea of *ha-olam haba.* It envisioned the resurrection of the body, a final judgment, restoration of all Jews to the land of Israel, and a rebuilding of the Temple in Jerusalem.

The Rabbis have no unified opinion on what this next world will look like, nor do they agree on the order of events which will transpire. The consensus seems to be that in the world-to-come all wrongs will be made right, the righteous rewarded, and the wicked punished. The body will come back to life, Israel will be restored, and the Temple rebuilt. And, significantly, the Rabbis declared that *all* Israel will have a share in the world-to-come (*Mishnah, Sanhedrin* 10:1).

The belief in the resurrection of the body after death is primarily of rabbinic origin. In the Bible, death is considered final for every individual. There is no bodily resurrection. Yet, there are a few biblical verses which talk about the restoration of *the national life of the people of Israel,* especially Ezekiel 37:11–14. Only the Book of Daniel, a very late document, makes a clear reference (12:2) to bodily resurrection:

> Many of those that sleep in the dust of the earth will awake, some to eternal life, others to reproaches, to everlasting abhorrence.

But while the Bible had a nebulous notion of life after death, the Rabbis considered resurrection of the body a cardinal belief for all Jews and sought evidence for it throughout the Bible. At times, they also interpreted texts quite fancifully in order to undergird their own understanding. For example, Rabbi Meir said:

> From where do we know that the resurrection of the body is derived from the Torah? As it is said, "Then will Moses and the children of Israel sing this song

unto the Lord" [Exod. 15:1]. It is not said "sang," but "will sing" [in the future]. This proves that the resurrection is deduced from the Torah.

(Babylonian Talmud, *Sanhedrin* 91b; for other examples see same page)

For many Rabbis, our world is an introduction to the next one:

Rabbi Jacob said: This world is like a corridor to the world-to-come; prepare yourself in the corridor, so that you may enter the hall.

(*Avot* 4:21)

With creative imagination, the Rabbis viewed the world-to-come as a place of peace and tranquility.

It was a favorite saying of Rab: This world is not like the world-to-come. In the world-to-come there is no eating or drinking; no giving birth to children or business transaction; no envy or hatred or rivalry; but the righteous sit enthroned, their crowns on their heads, and enjoy the brightness of the *Shechinah* [Divine Presence]. . . .

(*Berachot* 17a)

In Summary

The rabbinic notion of God builds upon the biblical idea and embellishes it with imagery and parable. Rabbinic theology is not systematic, but it does affirm that God exists and is One. The angels are God's messengers, but in no way do they diminish God's power or the capacity of every man and woman to pray directly to God. God is portrayed in anthropomorphic and anthropopathic terms, showing "justice" and "mercy," "loving" Israel and being loved in return. We see again the doctrine of Israel's chosenness. God is still a personal God, accessible to us and our prayers. For the first time, we find the idea of a Messiah who will restore the world to peace and righteousness, followed by an afterlife involving physical resurrection. Above all, we see the introduction of the notion of an Oral Law, divinely given, which made it possible for Judaism to grow and change in response to the challenges of a changing world.

3

PHILO'S SPIRITUAL

MONOTHEISM

Background

Thus far, we have examined two ways in which Jews of ancient times spoke of God. While there were significant differences between the God idea of the biblical Hebrews and that of the Rabbis, there were also great similarities.

We are probably most familiar with the biblical and rabbinic God ideas, for two reasons. Every time the Torah is read, we listen to the words of our biblical ancestors; and, since the *siddur* (prayer book) is in large measure a product of the rabbinic period, the prayers we recite express that way of relating to God.

Yet, few people know that great Jewish thinkers throughout the centuries had strikingly different notions about the nature of God. Philo Judaeus was one of them.

Philo Judaeus

When Alexander the Great conquered the Near East in the first half of the fourth century B.C.E., he brought with him, not only a powerful army, but also a dominant culture. Soon,

Egypt, Syria, and Judea, all fell under the influence of Greek civilization.

During this period, Alexandria, a city in northern Egypt, was the leading commercial and intellectual center as well as the chief meeting place of Greek and Oriental cultures. The largest library of the ancient world was found here. The city attracted the greatest minds of its time. Like their neighbors, Jews, who had been living in Alexandria since the third century B.C.E., were also influenced by the Greeks. In fact, Jews produced the first translation of the Bible, the Septuagint, a translation of the Bible into Greek, which became a cornerstone of Jewish-Greek culture.

Among the greatest thinkers of the Jews of Alexandria was Philo Judaeus, who lived from about 20 B.C.E. to 50 C.E. We have little information about his life. We know that he belonged to a very wealthy and influential Jewish family. His brother, Alexander, had an official position as alabarch, which meant that he collected taxes for the Romans. The Jewish historian Josephus records that this same Alexander donated all the silver and gold plates covering the nine gates of Herod's Temple. In other words, he was very rich. Philo, in addition to being a scholar, was also a diplomat. In the year 40 C.E., he led a delegation of the Jewish community to Emperor Caligula (Gaius Caesar) in Rome to protest the erection of statues of the emperor in Alexandrian synagogues. It appears that his appeal was successful, and the statues were finally removed.

Philo's Scholarship

Like other intellectuals of his time, Philo wrote in Greek. He knew science and philosophy. He also had an excellent background in Judaism, though scholars are not sure if, or to what extent, he knew Hebrew. He certainly was familiar with the Septuagint text of the Pentateuch and with the sermonic material and tradition of the synagogue. His writings were preserved by the Christian Church in the original Greek and in their Armenian translations.

Most of Philo's Jewish writings are in the form of biblical commentaries and can be divided into three categories:

1. For non-Jews who were interested in the study of Judaism, he wrote a group of texts which we can call exposition of the law, demonstrating that the ordinances of the Pentateuch are in harmony with the laws of nature.
2. For Jewish scholars, he wrote a number of essays which present a philosophical interpretation of the Torah.
3. His last series, entitled *Questions and Answers,* contains comments on specific biblical texts in the books of Genesis and Exodus and were intended for a more general audience.

Philo also produced purely philosophical and historical books. He was remarkably prolific, and his writings reflected both his own genius and the philosophical ideas of his time.

Philo's Synthesis of Judaism and Greek Culture

Living in a Greek environment, Philo tried to harmonize Judaism with the current intellectual movements of his time. When he interpreted the Bible, he read Greek philosophy into it by applying the then popular allegorical method. The Greek word *allegoria* means "to say another thing" and implies that, in addition to the obvious meaning of a text, there is a hidden meaning that needs to be uncovered.

For example, in his book *Questions and Answers,* he writes:

> Who are the three sons of Noah—Shem, Ham, and Japheth? [Gen. 5:32] These names are the symbols of three things in nature—of the good, the evil, and the indifferent; Shem is distinguished for good, Ham for evil, and Japheth for the indifferent.*
>
> ("On Genesis," I, 88)

Similarly, in the Book of Genesis we are told that the childless Sarah asked her husband, Abraham, to marry her maid Hagar in order to have a child with her (Gen. 15:2). Abraham did marry Hagar and fathered Ishmael. It was only later that Abraham and Sarah had a child of their own, named Isaac. For Philo this episode contains a much more profound message than its literal meaning. Abraham, says Philo, really stands for the "mind," Hagar for "school," Ishmael for "poor knowledge," Sarah for "wisdom," and Isaac for "joy." For Philo, the message of the Bible is that, when the mind (namely, an individual; here, Abraham) goes to school (Hagar), the result is poor knowledge (Ishmael). The accumulation of facts in the mind is not enough. What we need is wisdom. Therefore, when the mind (Abraham) finds wisdom (Sarah), the result is pure joy (Isaac). (See "On Genesis," III, 21.)

*All translations are taken from Loeb Classical Library, 1961.

Body and Soul

Like other Greek thinkers, Philo talked about the separation
between the soul and the body. In Greek thought, the universe, as a whole, and human beings, in particular, were made
up of two major components. The body, or matter, repre-
sented the perishable aspect of life and the source of all evil.
On the other hand, the soul, or the rational mind, stood for that
which is good, eternal, and unperishable.

Having accepted that separation in principle, Philo, as a Jew,
had a serious problem. In the Book of Genesis we read, "God
created man in His image" (1:27). If man is divided into body
and soul, and if man is created in God's image, does that mean
that God is also separated in two?

Philo declared that the answer was no. The term "image"
here, he said, refers to "mind." Therefore, it is after the pattern of the universal mind that our minds were created. As one
way of clarifying this dilemma, which he took very seriously,
Philo built a system called "spiritual monotheism."

Spiritual Monotheism

1. God Is One

Philo, like other Jewish thinkers, proclaimed the unity of
God. On the biblical passage, "It is not good for man to be
alone" (Gen. 2:18), he comments:

> God is alone: a Unity, in the sense that His nature
> is single, not composite, whereas each one of us
> and of all other created beings is made up of many
> things. . . . But God is not a composite being, consist-
> ing of many parts. . . .
>
> ("Allegories of Sacred Laws," II, i)

2. We Cannot Describe God

Philo's God is far above and beyond our universe, or "transcendent" in philosophical terms. Though the human mind is able to understand something about God's *activities* in the world, such as the workings of nature which we can see with our own eyes, God as an entity remains totally beyond our limited comprehension. God is different from us in every conceivable way. Therefore, God cannot be defined in human terms, nor can God be described by language. God is simply unknowable. In fact, Philo argues that "God alone has an accurate knowledge of God's own nature."

According to Philo, God is the "Soul" of the universe, the universal Mind, the greatest cause of everything there is. Even though beyond both time and place, God totally fills the universe.

3. God Cannot Be Named

Philo declared that it is impossible to give a precise name to God, as is done in the Bible and rabbinic literature. Our language, he declared, is not capable of covering all the aspects of God in one term. The best that we can do, said Philo, is to refer to God as *Ontos,* a Greek term, meaning "Being," "That which exists."

At times, we direct our prayer to the God of Abraham, God of Isaac, and God of Jacob. We even say that God is "good," "just," or "holy." This, however, is really our way of speaking *about* God. In reality, God is more than "good" or "holy." No name, attribute, or characteristic does complete justice to what God is. Philo tells us that the only attributes we can safely apply to God are not the positive ones, but the negative ones. For example, to say that God is "holy" is simply inadequate. For this description would limit God to *our* idea of holiness. The most we can say is that "God is *not unholy*" or "God is *not unjust.*" We will see this same idea asserted in the philosophy of another great Jewish thinker, Maimonides.

4. We Can Prove That God Exists

Philo was one of the first Jewish thinkers to raise the question of God's existence. He asked the question outright: "How do we know that God really exists?" In response, Philo advanced a number of arguments already known in his own time. Two of his major proofs were as follows:

a. God as the universal Mind:

Just as a person has a mind, so does the universe have a Mind. Just as the human mind controls the body, so does the universal Mind, God, control the universe.

> Your reason will show you that as there is a mind in you, so is there in the universe; and that as your mind has taken upon itself sovereign control of all that is in you, and brought every part into subjection to itself, so too He . . . guides and controls the universe by law and right of an absolute way.
>
> ("The Migration of Abraham," 33)

b. The teleological argument:

Philo's second proof is the so-called "teleological" argument. (The word *telos* in Greek means "purpose," "design," "order.") It is based on the observation that there is an order in the universe. This order implies the existence of an organizing Mind behind it, and that is God.

> When one enters a well-ordered city in which the arrangements for civil life are very admirably managed, what else will he suppose but that this city is directed by good rulers? So, then, he who comes to the truly Great City, this world, and beholds hills and plains teeming with animals and plants, the rivers . . . the seas . . . the air . . . the sun and the moon . . . and the whole firmament revolving in rhythmic order, must he not naturally or rather necessarily gain

the conception of the Maker and Father and Ruler also? For none of the works of human art is self-made . . . surely it has been wrought by One of excellent knowledge and absolute perfection [that is, God].

("Special Laws," I, 6)

5. Though God Does Not Have a Body, God Controls the Material World

Philo insisted that God is absolute and beyond the limits of human knowledge. Yet, at the same time, he argued that God knows everything that goes on in the universe and shows great care for its well-being. The challenge of explaining the relationship between God (who does not have a body) and the material world has been a problem for many thinkers throughout the centuries. How does God, as pure intelligence, communicate with material things? If God is spiritual and perfect, where does perishable matter come from?

In the Bible as well as in rabbinic literature, there were attempts to resolve this problem. One way was to present angels as messengers of God. Another approach was to personify certain aspects of God as if they were independent entities. Thus, for example, in Psalms 33:6, we read, "By the word of the Lord the heavens were made. . . ." This verse implies that the "word" is a being in itself. Another example of personification in the Bible is "wisdom." In the Book of Proverbs we read, "Wisdom has built her house, / She has hewn her seven pillars" (9:1).

In both of these examples, the "word" of God and "wisdom" have been personified as if they were separate entities, operating at the command of God.

6. The Logos: Philo's Answer

Philo taught that God operates in the world through the personified *logos,* a Greek term which means "word" or "speech."

What exactly is this logos? To understand what Philo meant

by this word, we first need to know something about Plato's theory of forms. For it was by reinterpreting Plato's theory that Philo advanced his own concept.

According to Plato, a prominent Greek philosopher of the fourth century B.C.E., everything in our world is a copy of the perfect essence or form of that particular object. The object itself is perishable, but the essence, or form, is eternal. Thus, for example, people live and die, but the essence of a "human being" is eternal. Similarly, there are many different sizes and shapes of "chairs" or "tables," but the essence of a "chair" or a "table" is timeless. These eternal patterns are part of a "heaven of forms" which exists independently of any knowing mind. These forms are even independent of God. Therefore, God, who has no body, contemplates the essence and creates the object.

Philo was influenced by Plato's theory of forms but could not accept these forms as eternal patterns existing *outside* God. That acceptance might have led to dualism, a belief that, in addition to God, there is another force equal to God operating in the world. Since Philo was a strict monotheist, he rejected any notion that might compromise God's unity. He, therefore, used Plato's theory of forms, asserted that these forms indeed existed, but maintained that they were not eternal, since they were actually created by God.

For Philo, forms have three kinds of existence. They first appear as thoughts growing out of God's essence. Next, they are created as bodyless or incorporeal beings. Finally, they turn into independent powers and operate within the world as God's agents.

According to Philo, the total progression of these forms is called the logos. The logos bridges the gap between our perfect God and the imperfect and finite world of people and matter.

Unfortunately, Philo does not give us a more precise definition of logos. He refers to the logos as the totality of forms, as God's chief power, as the instrument of creation. He also identifies it with the Torah, with wisdom, and with the highest of angels.

Because Philo's God is too exalted to come in contact with impure matter, it is through the logos that God operates in the world. The logos, therefore, stands between God and the universe and enables the spiritual God to affect the material world.

To put it another way, it is through the logos that Philo's "transcendent God" (a God who is beyond the universe) can become an "immanent God" (a God who is in close relationship with the world).

7. The Logos Is Not a Person

Philo never considered this logos a human being. It is only in later Christian writings that the logos was identified with Jesus, as when we read in the Christian Bible: "In the beginning was the Word, and the Word was with God, and the Word was God. . . . And the Word became flesh and dwelt among us . . ." (John 1:1, 14).

That is one important area where Judaism and Christianity parted company in matters of belief.

8. We Can Approach God

According to Philo, our body belongs to the world of the senses, to the world of matter, which is evil, a view that was shared by few other Jewish thinkers. On the other hand, our reason, which is really part of the divine logos, gives us the potential to dwell in the spiritual world. The goal of every individual should be to free himself or herself from the shackles of the body and of material things and to reach out for the Soul of the universe, which is God.

The Bible talks about "cities of refuge" (Num. 35:9–15; Deut. 4:41–42) that were to be established in order to provide a safe place for someone who unintentionally killed another person. In his allegorical commentary, Philo says that the real purpose of this biblical text is to identify, not cities, but a number of stages which the human mind has to cross as it moves from the world of matter towards God. The final goal is to reach "the Supreme Divine Word, who is the Fountain of Wisdom, in order that he may draw from the stream and, released from death, gain life eternal as his prize" ("On Flight and Finding," 18).

9. God and Israel

For Philo, the Jews who lived in Israel as well as those who lived in colonies outside of the Holy Land constituted "one nation." God has a special relation with this nation as a whole. The gift of having a vision of God, declares Philo, was given not only to Moses but to the entire nation of Israel. In fact, the name Israel, he argues, means "seeing God" (as it were, from the Hebrew *ra-ah,* to see, and *El,* God).

Furthermore, the revelation of the Torah was God's special gift to Israel, for Israel has been favored by God with the highest level of prophecy, prophecy by divine voice at Mt. Sinai.

10. The Problem of Evil

Philo denies that God is the cause of evil. The evils of the world come from the world of matter. Yet, he admits, under certain circumstances evil does emerge from God, as in the case of the Egyptians, at the time of the Exodus, upon whom God directly inflicted punishment.

In discussing the suffering of the righteous, Philo basically followed the teachings of the rabbinic Sages of his time, arguing that sometimes the righteous suffer because they are not perfect in their righteousness. Sometimes, evil is only a test of faithfulness; at times, people suffer not because of their sins but because of the misdeeds of their ancestors. Like other philosophers, however, Philo urged all human beings to practice virtue for its own sake, for this leads to happiness.

In Summary

Philo borrows freely from Plato's theory of forms, but he adapts it in accordance with his deeply-held Jewish convictions. His theological system can be termed "spiritual monotheism." For Philo, God cannot be described. The best that we can do with our inadequate language is to say what God is not. God is one and can only be referred to as *Ontos.* God exists yet is unknowable. Through the logos it is possible for God, who is pure spirit, to have contact with the impure world. God has a special relationship with Israel (the name *Israel* meaning "seeing God") as exemplified by God's revelation of Torah at Mount Sinai. Our ultimate goal should be to reach the Soul of the universe, which is God. This can be done through the fullest development of our reason, which is really part of the divine logos. Evil is a consequence of the imperfection of the world and is not related to God.

4

THE NEO-ARISTOTELIANISM

OF MAIMONIDES

Background

Philo was only one of several Jewish philosophers who drew inspiration from Greek thought and culture. While Philo felt a spiritual bond with the ideas of Plato, another Jewish thinker, Maimonides, built on the writings of the Greek philosopher Aristotle.

Maimonides was one of the most illustrious Jewish scholars of the Middle Ages. Known in rabbinic circles as Rambam (an acronym made up of the first initials of his full name, *R*abbi *M*oses *B*en *M*aimon), he is recognized as one of the most brilliant scholars in all of Jewish history. Indeed, of him it was said: "From Moses [of the Bible] to Moses [Maimonides] there was none like Moses [Maimonides]."

Maimonides was born in Cordoba, Spain, in 1135, the son of a famous *dayyan* (member of a rabbinic court). When a fanatic Moslem group called the Almohades took over Cordoba in 1148, Maimonides and his family fled for fear of religious persecution. They wandered from place to place and, finally, settled in Fez, Morocco, in 1160. It was during these trying days that Maimonides began to write his major works.

In 1165, the family left Fez, traveled to Acre in Palestine,

and finally settled in Fostat, the old city of Cairo. Initially, Maimonides dedicated himself to pursuing his scholarly interests. When his brother died, however, he had to take over the responsibility of caring for his family. He became a doctor and was appointed court physician to Saladin, the vizier of Egypt. While his main livelihood was practicing medicine, Maimonides continued to write books of great importance. In time, because of his reputation, he was also designated the official head of the Jewish community of Fostat. When he died in 1204, the entire Jewish world mourned for him. His remains were taken to Tiberias in Palestine for burial, and his grave is still visited by many pilgrims.

The Influence of Maimonides

Maimonides' influence on future generations of Jewish and non-Jewish thinkers was tremendous. Even those who did not totally agree with him recognized his greatness. He had a vast store of knowledge, an unusual ability to express difficult concepts in simple language, and a remarkable skill at presenting the rabbinic and philosophic literature of his time in a clear and orderly manner.

Maimonides was a rationalist. Basically, a rationalist holds that the world can be explained in a logical manner and that the human mind is one of the most important avenues for knowing and approaching God. Therefore, Maimonides' writings reflect this approach, along with an attempt to reconcile Judaism with Greek philosophy, particularly with the teachings of Aristotle and his disciples.

The Books of Maimonides

Maimonides wrote extensively, not only Jewish texts, but also essays on medicine, astronomy, and logic. More than four hundred of his responsa are still available. Responsa are answers to questions from people seeking to determine what Jewish law has to say about contemporary problems not explicitly mentioned in the Talmud or other legal texts. Only great scholars, Maimonides among them, were entrusted with the responsibility of issuing these legal opinions, which often became law.

Maimonides' major works are: *The Commentary to the Mishnah*, written originally in Arabic; his *Book of the Commandments*, where he analyzed the 613 *mitzvot*; and his monumental *Mishneh Torah* (The Repetition of the Torah) where he arranged in fourteen volumes the entire corpus of rabbinic law in a systematic fashion.

His major philosophical book is *The Guide to the Perplexed*, written in Arabic around the year 1200 for his star pupil, Joseph ben Junah ibn Shamun. In this book, he addresses himself not to beginners but to the intellectual elite.

My speech in the present treatise is directed . . . to one who has philosophized and has knowledge of the true sciences.

(*Guide,** int. to part I)

The Theology of Maimonides

While a number of his opinions on matters of belief are found in much simpler language in other writings prepared for the general public, it is in the *Guide* that Maimonides presents his full theological position. Elements of that position include the following:

1. God Is a Simple Being, Exists, and Has No Body

Maimonides proclaimed a spiritual concept of God. He followed the Greek philosopher, Aristotle (384–322 B.C.E.), who had spoken of God as a simple being, a pure intellect, whose major activity is thinking thoughts. Like Aristotle, Maimonides, too, maintained that God exists and that God is one and incorporeal, that is, without a body.

In his *Commentary to the Mishnah,* where he formulates his Thirteen Principles of Faith, Maimonides speaks of God in these terms:

> He is the cause of all existence. In Him all else subsists and from Him derives. . . . He is sufficient to himself. . . . God is one, the cause of all oneness. . . . He is incorporeal [has no body]. . . . [God] is absolutely eternal.
>
> (*Helek: Sanhedrin,* chap. 10)

---

*All quotes from the *Guide* are taken from *The Guide to the Perplexed,* trans. S. Pines; Chicago: University of Chicago, 1963. Other quotes are taken from I. Twersky, *A Maimonides Reader;* New York: Behrman, 1972.

2. God's Existence Can Be Proven: The Cosmological Argument

How do we know that God exists? Maimonides repeats Aristotle's "cosmological" argument. The "proof" begins with the observation that every object in the world is moved by another. When, for example, Z moves, it is because it is affected by Y; and Y causes the move, because of the impact of X. This, however, cannot go on forever. Ultimately, there must be a being which starts the process of motion, without being moved itself. This first "unmoved mover" is God. In the words of Maimonides:

> It is as if you say: this stone, which was in motion, was moved by a staff; the staff was moved by a hand; the hand by tendons; the tendons by muscles; the muscles by nerves; the nerves by natural heat; and the natural heat by the form that subsists therein, this form being undoubtedly the first mover.
>
> (*Guide*, II, 1)

If one were to project this movement all the way up to the cosmic scene, one would end up with a universal mover—and that is God.

3. The Doctrine of Attributes

Maimonides argued that philosophy and correct reasoning enable us to prove the existence of God. However, he cautioned that it is beyond the capacity of the human mind to comprehend the totality of God.

> God's essence as it really is, the human mind does not understand and is incapable of grasping or investigating.
>
> (*Mishneh Torah*, Knowledge, Basic Principles, 1:9)

The reason for this lack of understanding is our own limitations.

> Human reason cannot fully conceive God in His true essence, because of the perfection of God's essence and the imperfection of our own reason.
> (*Mishnah, Avot,* Eight Chapters, VIII)

So what can we know of God? Maimonides maintained that God is a simple being. Here the word "simple" does not mean naive, or uncomplicated. It signifies that God is not made of multiple entities.

God is not made of any material "stuff" which can be created and destroyed. Yet, we often refer to God as if God possessed a physical body. For example, in the Bible, we find many references to God's "feet" (Exod. 24:10), God's "finger" (Exod. 31:18), God's "hand" (Exod. 9:3). If God is a spiritual being, how do we explain these terms? Maimonides was concerned that unthinking people would take these expressions literally and believe that God is corporeal, that is, having a body. So, he writes:

> All these expressions are adapted to the mental capacity of the majority of mankind who have a clear perception of physical bodies only. The Torah speaks in the language of men. All these phrases are metaphorical.
> (*Mishneh Torah,* Knowledge, Basic Principles, 1:9)

Maimonides wants us to understand that when the Bible says, "God saw," this does not mean that God witnessed events with physical eyes; the verb "saw" here is figurative for intellectual comprehension. It is seeing through the mind. Also, God's "place" does not refer to a physical location, but to God's existence. Similarly, God's "throne" signifies the greatness of God, and so on.

At times, God is spoken of as being "angry," or "merciful." These, too, should not be taken literally. Otherwise, we would have to assume that God moves from one mood to another, from "anger" to "mercy." This, however, would imply change and multiplicity within God, which is not acceptable. When the term "angry" or "merciful" is used about human beings and God, Maimonides reminds us, they do not mean the same thing. These words are not different in degree, they are different in kind. Thus, for example, when we say that God is "merciful," this is to be understood from our own human perspective. We know what it is to be "merciful," but there is no such thing in God which would correspond to the term "merciful."

These problems led Maimonides to formulate a "doctrine of attributes." According to Maimonides, as Philo before him, nothing positive can be said of God. The reason is because God is a simple being, and any positive attribute, such as "eternal," "powerful," or "wise," would imply that these qualities are, as it were, "added" to the simple nature of God, making God a composite being.

When we state that God is a "living God," we must remember, Maimonides would say, that God "lives" but not through an added "life." Similarly, God "knows," but not through knowledge; God is "wise," but not through wisdom.

The attributes that can possibly be applied to God are those which derive from God's effects on us. These must be understood properly. For example, "God is merciful" simply means that God *acts* mercifully; "God is just" simply means that God *acts* justly; "God is powerful" simply means that God *acts* powerfully.

The only real attributes of God, especially those that deal with God's essence, are the negative attributes. Thus, for example, when we state that "God is," we do not mean to say that God's "existence" is "added" to what God is; we simply mean that God is "not non-existent." When we state that "God is one," we do not imply that "oneness" is "added" to God; we simply mean to say that "God is not many," or that "God has no equal."

> The meaning is that He has no equal, and not that the notion of oneness attaches to His essence.
>
> *(Guide,* I, 57)

4. God Created the World Out of Nothing

Maimonides followed the Aristotelians when he discussed the existence and the nature of God, but he disagreed with them on the creation of the world. Aristotle had taught that God, as the Unmoved Mover of the universe, represents the highest purpose, the highest good in life. Just as an object of desire (for example, a beautiful picture, an ideal) attracts and causes motion, everything in the universe moves toward the Final Mover, God. God, Aristotle added, is not a creator. The world is eternal and, therefore, not subject to origin and destruction.

Maimonides took exception with the Aristotelians on this issue. He maintained, as the Bible and rabbinic literature did before him, that the world was freely created by God *ex nihilo* (out of nothing). He felt that Aristotle's opinion about the origin of the world was not convincing. The doctrine of creation, he argued, is not impossible. It can be defended on philosophical terms. In fact, it has the least amount of objections to it.

For example, in the Aristotelian system, where God is viewed as pure thought, only another pure thought can emerge from God. Maimonides then asked: If this is the case, where does matter come from? His answer: It comes out of God's will. It comes because God formed it. The physical world is the product of God's own free will.

Similarly, if we were to accept the Aristotelian doctrine of the eternity and absolute changelessness of the world, then we would have to give up the miracles of the Bible. Miracles only take place when God interrupts the course of nature for the

benefit of someone; and that is only possible when the world
is seen as being formed and ruled by God. If the world is
eternal and functions on its own, without God's control, there
can be no miracles. Mechanical causation and miracles are,
therefore, incompatible.

Even though Maimonides talked about miracles, he understood them differently from others. According to him, God
does not interfere in the workings of nature. All the so-called
miracles were built into the process of creation at the very
beginning of time so that, when the appropriate circumstances
appeared right, the "miracle" took place.

Another argument which Maimonides advanced against the
eternality of the world is that mechanical necessity as the explanation for the existence of the world would make prayer,
free will, prophecy, the chosenness of Israel, and other such
notions impossible.

The doctrine of creation, therefore, would be preferable to
the doctrine of eternity, because it allows us to answer many
questions more satisfactorily regarding the operation of the
universe as a whole.

5. Angels Are God's Messengers

Like other rabbis before him, Maimonides, too, believed in
the existence of angels, but he identified them with the "pure
intellects" of the Aristotelian system.

Aristotle had taught that between God and the world there
are a number of spheres which move in a circle and never stop.
Each of these spheres (which include various planets) is gifted
with reason or intellect. Aristotle counted as many as fifty
spheres rotating around our world, which he considered standing at the center of the universe. In the thinking of Maimonides, these intellects are really "angels."

> He [Aristotle] speaks of separate intellects and we
> speak of angels.
>
> (*Guide,* II, 6)

The basic meaning of the word "angel" in Hebrew—Maimonides reminds us—is "messenger." Primarily, these angels do God's bidding on earth.

> Our Law does not deny the fact that He, may He be exalted, governs that which exists here through the intermediation of the angels.
>
> (Ibid.)

That God rules the world through these angels, writes Maimonides, is made clear in the Bible as well. We read, for example, "Let us make man in our image" (Gen. 1:26), or "Let us, then, go down and confound their speech" (Gen. 11:7). In these texts, says Maimonides, God is really addressing the angels. (See Babylonian Talmud, *Sanhedrin* 38b.)

It is important to remember that these angels are not human beings. They do not have bodies. They are pure intellects. Maimonides writes:

> All forces are angels.
>
> (*Guide*, 11, 6)

How do these angels function? Maimonides mentions the case of birth as an example:

> God has placed in the sperm a formative force shaping the limbs and giving them configuration, and . . . this force is the angel.
>
> (Ibid.)

The difference between Aristotle and Maimonides on this subject is as follows:

> His [Aristotle's] belief [is] that all these things [namely, the intellects] are eternal and that they pro-

ceed necessarily from Him. . . . We ourselves believe that . . . it was He [that is, God] who created the intellects and the spheres and put in them the governing forces.

(Ibid.)

6. Evil Is the Result of an Imperfect World and Human Actions

Maimonides rejects the idea that God can be the source of evil in the world. God is only good, and from good only good can come out.

All good things must exist in God and with regard to Him all deficiencies must be denied.

(*Guide,* III, 19)

For Maimonides, evil is simply the denial of good. Some of this evil is self-inflicted, as when one person hurts another. Other types of evil exist because the world is made of matter which is subject to genesis and decay.

7. We Have Free Will

Maimonides strongly argues that human beings are blessed with free will. This concept constitutes the very foundation of our Torah.

. . . Man's conduct is entirely in his own hands. . . . Were a man compelled to act according to the dictates of predestination, then the commands and prohibitions of the Law would become null and void and the Law would be completely false, since man would have no freedom of choice in what he does.

(*Mishnah, Avot,* Eight Chapters, VIII)

Similarly:

> Every human being may become righteous like Moses
> our Teacher, or wicked like Jeroboam; wise or foolish,
> merciful or cruel.
>
> (*Mishneh Torah,* Knowledge, Repentance, 3:2)

Even the rabbinic saying, "All is in the hands of heaven
except the fear of heaven" (*Berachot* 33b; *Niddah* 16b; *Megil-
lah* 25a), does not contradict this teaching, says Maimonides.

> By the word "all" the Rabbis meant to designate only
> natural phenomena which are not influenced by the
> will of man, as whether a person is tall or short,
> whether it is rainy or dry, whether the air is pure
> or impure, and all other such things that happen
> in the world, which have no connection with man's
> conduct.
>
> (*Mishnah, Avot,* Eight Chapters, VIII)

At this point a question needs to be raised. If God already has
foreknowledge of my actions, how can I be free? To this
Maimonides responds by stating that there is no resemblance
between our knowledge and God's knowledge. The word
"knowledge," when applied to humanity and God, does not
mean the same thing. We do not exactly understand what and
how God "knows."

> [God] realizes His true being, and knows it as it is, not
> with a knowledge external to himself, as is our knowl-
> edge. For our knowledge and ourselves are separate.
> But as for the Creator . . . His knowledge and His life
> are one. . . . If the Creator lived as other living crea-
> tures live, and His knowledge were external to him-
> self, there would be a plurality of deities, namely, He

himself, His life, and His knowledge. . . . This, however, is not so. He is One in every aspect. . . .
(*Mishneh Torah,* Knowledge, Basic Principles, 2:10)

We find the same thought expressed in the following
quote:

God does not know by means of knowledge and does
not live by means of life. . . . He is the knowledge, the
knower, and the known.
(*Mishnah, Avot,* Eight Chapters, VIII)

In other words, God is very different from us.

If the human reason could grasp His knowledge, it
would be able also to define His essence, since both
are one and the same. . . . All that we comprehend is
that just as we know that God exists, so are we cogni-
zant of the fact that He knows. If we are asked, "What
is the nature of God's knowledge?" we answer that we
do not know any more than we know the nature of His
true existence.
(Ibid.)

8. Our Goal in Life: Intellectual and Spiritual Perfection

For Maimonides, the highest goals in life are intellectual and
spiritual perfection as well as the contemplation of God. We
have been given the power to rule over matter which is the
source of all corruption. Each of us has a number of impulses
—some good and some bad. Our job is to control them, restrict
their destructive efforts, and channel them toward good
ends.

In the *Mishneh Torah,* Maimonides, borrowing a popular
Greek notion, suggested that whatever we do we ought to do
in moderation. We should "aim at the happy medium" (Knowledge, 1:4). However, in the *Guide,* he went further to argue

that we should pursue only that which is absolutely indispensable.

> It behooves him who prefers to be a human being in truth, not a beast having the shape and configuration of a human being, to endeavor to diminish all the impulses of matter—such as eating, drinking, sex, anger . . . and all the habits consequent upon desire and anger—to be ashamed of them, and to set for them limits in his soul.
>
> (*Guide*, III, 8)

All the commandments and prohibitions of the Torah are intended to help us quell these negative impulses.

For Maimonides the ideal conduct for any person is as follows:

> The greater a man is the more scrupulous should he be in all such things, and do more than the strict letter of the Law requires. And if a man has been scrupulous in his conduct, gentle in his conversation, pleasant toward his fellow creatures, affable in manner when receiving them, not retorting, even when affronted, but showing courtesy to all, even to those who treat him with disdain, conducting his commercial affairs with integrity, not readily accepting the hospitality of the ignorant nor frequenting their company, not seen at all times, but devoting himself to the study of the Torah, wrapped in *talit,* and crowned with phylacteries, and doing more than his duty in all things, avoiding, however, extremes and exaggerations—such a man has sanctified God and, concerning him, Scripture says [SJV/Isa. 49:3], "And He said to me, 'You are My servant, O Israel, in whom I will be glorified.' "
>
> (*Mishneh Torah,* Knowledge, Basic Principles, 5:11)

In Summary

Maimonides was deeply influenced by the writing of Aristotle. A rationalist, he subjected every assertion to the tests of logic.

Maimonides believed that God was a simple being, One, with no body, whose existence could be demonstrated using the cosmological argument.

God is pure intellect, the Unmoved Mover of the universe. The attributes of God are only metaphors, understood by our limited mind and expressed in human terminology.

God created the world out of nothing. Therefore, though God is pure intellect, God affects the world through angels, pure intellects who are the product of God's will.

Evil comes from human misuse of free will and from the inherent imperfection of the material world. Our goal, therefore, must be intellectual and spiritual perfection.

5

THE MYSTICISM OF LURIA

Background

Mystics strive to achieve communion with God through meditation, prayer, and fasting. They yearn for their souls to rise towards heaven, to unite their earthly "selves" with God. They believe that God can be reached or experienced directly through one's heart, through emotion, without recourse to reason or empirical evidence.

Judaism has had a long tradition of mysticism. Though called by different names—including *sitre Torah* (secrets of the Torah), *chochmah penimit* (inner wisdom), and *derech ha-emet* (the way of truth)—it became known, from the fourteenth century on, as Kabbalah. Accordingly, the sages involved in this pursuit were called "Kabbalists."

We do not know precisely when mysticism began in Jewish life, though it probably originated in rabbinic times. The early rabbis, however, were not very supportive of mystical speculation, fearing that it could lead people away from Judaism. In fact, they painted a grim scenario for those who dared to engage in mystical pursuits:

Four persons entered the *pardes* ["orchard," that is,

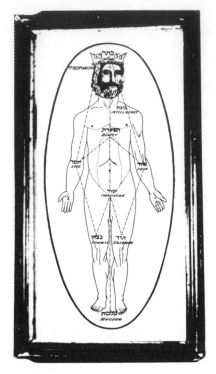

field of mysticism]. . . . Ben Azzai cast a look and died.
. . . Ben Zoma looked and became demented. . . .
Acher ["Another," name given to Elisha ben Abuyah]
cut down the plants [that is, became estranged from
Judaism]. . . . Rabbi Akiba alone departed unhurt.

(*Hagigah*, 14b)

Consequently, they taught:

. . . The mysteries of the chariot [Ezek. 1:4ff.] may not
be taught even to one [person], unless he is a sage and
can grasp it on his own understanding. Whoever
speculates upon four things, a pity for him! . . . [That
is:] What is above [heaven], what is below [the nether-
world], what is before [the creation of the world], and
what is after [the end of days].

(Ibid. 2:1)

These subjects were so sensitive that the ancient rabbis felt that they should be approached with great caution, and only then by those who had the intellectual capacity, as well as the powers of concentration, to pay total attention to the teacher's words. We read in the Talmud:

> When two sit before their master, one engages in discussion with his master and the other inclines his ear to the instruction; but [when there are] three [students], one engages in discussion with his master, and the other two engage in discussion with one another and do not know what their master is saying.
>
> (Ibid. 11b)

Commenting on the Mishnaic passage which limits the study of the mysteries of creation to only two students (*Hagigah* 2:1), one rabbi said: "Two" means only two students, and certainly not three. Another went further: "Two" means the teacher and the student alone.

Early Mystical Concerns

In spite of these stark cautions, those select few who engaged in mysticism produced a vast literature through the centuries. The literature can be divided into two broad periods: classical and postclassical.

Early Kabbalists were concerned with questions of origin, such as: How was the world created? Where did we come from? They believed that if we knew the mystery of the "ladder of ascent" (that is, the order of creation), which connects the created world to God, it would be possible for us to ascend and return to God. They, therefore, speculated on the mystery of creation *(ma-aseh bereshit)*. One of the most influential books written at the end of the classical period was *The Zohar*.

The Zohar

The Zohar, the masterpiece of Spanish kabbalism, is often called "The Bible of the Mystics." It is widely assumed that it was written in the 1280s by Moses ben Shem Tov de Leon, in Guadalajara, a small town northeast of Madrid. De Leon himself, however, attributed the writing to a great rabbinic sage who lived in the second century C.E., Rabbi Simeon bar Yohai. A legend holds that the book was hidden in a cave in ancient Israel, where Simeon and his son Eliezer hid from the Romans for thirteen years. According to legend, someone discovered the book many years thereafter and sent it to his own son in Catalonia. A great wind, however, miraculously lifted the book and brought it to Aragon, where it fell into the hands of de Leon.

The primary aim of *The Zohar* is to explain the *mitzvot* in a mystical way and to encourage the performance of *mitzvot* for mystical purposes. Written mostly in Aramaic, it takes the form of a collection of long and short *midrashim* (plural of *midrash*) on various portions of the Torah. Through commentaries on specific texts, it deals with the "hidden" meanings of the particular Torah portions, the explanations of the mysteries of the soul, the mysterious powers attributed to the Hebrew alphabet, the profound nature of God, the kabbalistic significance of the Ten Commandments, and other similar subjects.

The Postclassical Period—Isaac Luria

With the appearance of *The Zohar,* Jewish mysticism began to spread to European countries outside of Spain. From the fourteenth through the eighteenth century, a number of mystical books were written. Finally, the kabbalistic movement was firmly established in Safed, a city in the Galilee. Among the leaders was a brilliant thinker by the name of Rabbi Isaac Luria

Ashkenazi, who not only superseded his own masters but left a lasting mark on the future development of Kabbalah.

In kabbalistic literature, Isaac Luria is often referred to as Ha-Ari (The Lion), from the Hebrew initials of the words *Ha-Elohi Rabbi Yitzhak* (The Divine Rabbi Isaac). He was born in Jerusalem in the year 1534. His father, born in Poland (some say in Germany), came to Jerusalem where he married into a well-to-do Sephardic family. After his father's death, Luria's mother took young Isaac to Cairo, Egypt, to live with her brother, a wealthy tax collector. At the age of fifteen, Isaac married his uncle's daughter, then started his studies of Kabbalah under the guidance of famous scholars. He began to lead an ascetic, solitary life, frequently traveling alone to an island near Cairo for long periods of meditation. About the year 1570, he came to Palestine and settled in Safed with his family. There, he became the student of Moses Cordobero, one of the most learned kabbalistic thinkers of the time.

Luria's reputation grew. People spoke of him as a man possessed by the "holy spirit." Some claimed that he had received special "revelations from the prophet Elijah." Others, especially Luria's students, alluded to the possibility that Luria considered himself "the Messiah, the son of Joseph," the forerunner of the Messiah of the Davidic family.

Rabbi Isaac Luria died in 1572, at the age of thirty-eight, just a few years after he had moved to Safed. Unfortunately, he wrote very little, for he felt that he lacked the ability to set down his thoughts in a systematic fashion. Therefore, it was left to a few of his most brilliant students to promulgate his teachings. Among these pupils was Hayyim Vital Calabrese (1534–1620), whose memory and subsequent transcription of Luria's lectures assured his teacher a prominent place in the annals of Jewish thought.

God in the Kabbalah

Kabbalah is not a single system of thought, but rather a particular approach to considering the mystery of life. Indeed, different Kabbalists have come up with various doctrines, often totally contradictory. Yet, there are some basic notions on which most Kabbalists would agree.

1. God Exists but Is Unknowable

At the center of Kabbalah stands a belief in God. Kabbalists maintain that God is totally unknowable to the human mind. All we can say is that God is unlimited and infinite. God is usually referred to as *En Sof* (The Endless One) or, in the flowery language of *The Zohar,* as "The hidden of all hidden." Only by observing the beauty and order of our physical world can we derive the existence of this *En Sof.*

The Kabbalists assert that there is a constant interaction between the celestial kingdom and our universe. Everything in our world has a counterpart in the world above. In fact, when creation took place it occurred on both levels simultaneously. Therefore, every movement here below causes a corresponding movement above.

> This world is formed on the pattern of the world above, and whatever takes place in this earthly realm occurs also in the realm above.
> (*The Zohar,* II, 144a, vol. IV, p.8; Soncino, 1956)

And conversely:

> Power below depends on the corresponding power above.
> (*The Zohar,* I, 144b, vol. II, p. 65)

The Kabbalists also taught that knowledge about God's relationship to the world is attainable through meditation, prayer, and contemplation.

2. Manifestations of God: The Ten Sefirot

How is God manifested in the world and the human mind? To bridge the gap between the unknowable God and the known universe, Kabbalah teaches that between God and the world are ten *sefirot,* divine luminaries or spheres, through which God is revealed. Through these *sefirot,* say the Kabbalists, the world came into being and is preserved. The names of the ten *sefirot* are: *Keter* (Crown), *Chochmah* (Wisdom), *Binah* (Understanding), *Chesed* (Mercy), *Din* or *Gevurah* (Judgment or Power), *Tiferet* (Beauty), *Netzach* (Eternity), *Hod* (Majesty), *Yesod* (Foundation) and *Malchut* (Kingdom).

The ten *sefirot* form a hierarchy: *Keter,* the first and the highest of all the *sefirot,* is at the top and considered to be the closest to *En Sof.* The lowest is *Malchut,* also called *Shechinah,* a female symbol, representing the Divine Presence in the universe and the point of contact between our world and the upper spheres. Each of the *sefirot* also has other names and numerous symbolic associations.

The chart on the following page shows the ten *sefirot* as conceived by most of the Kabbalists.

3. The Ten Sefirot and Man

The Kabbalists taught that the human body is a microcosm of the universe. Therefore, all manifestations in the universe must symbolically assume human form.

> What, then, is man? Does he consist solely of skin, flesh, bones, and sinews? Nay, the essence of man is his soul. . . . Man is something inward. . . . The man below corresponds entirely to the Man above.
>
> (*The Zohar,* II, 76a, vol. III, pp. 230–31)

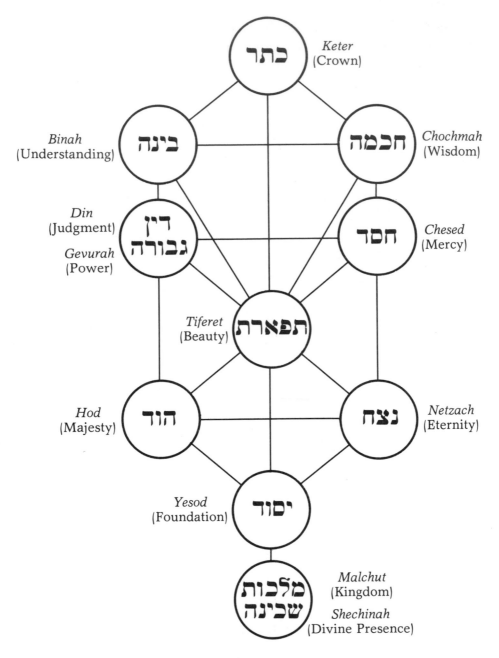

Keter
(Crown)

Binah
(Understanding)

Chochmah
(Wisdom)

Din
(Judgment)

Gevurah
(Power)

Chesed
(Mercy)

Tiferet
(Beauty)

Hod
(Majesty)

Netzach
(Eternity)

Yesod
(Foundation)

Malchut
(Kingdom)

Shechinah
(Divine Presence)

Based on *Back to the Sources,* ed. Barry W. Holtz, p.321; New York: Summit Books, 1984.

The "upper" and the "lower" worlds find their meeting point in us. We represent the Divine Presence on earth.

Luria's Teachings

Luria assumed many basic kabbalistic beliefs, but he also introduced quite a few innovations of great importance. His theory of creation is among his greatest contributions.

There are three stages in Luria's idea of creation:

1. Tzimtzum (Contraction)—A Self-Limiting God

Before Luria, the Kabbalists argued that the world was created as a result of a series of emanations coming from God, who filled the world. Luria disagreed. He taught that, if God filled the world, there would have been no room for anything else. Therefore in order to make the physical world possible, God pulled back and contracted. This retreat of God is called by Luria *tzimtzum* (contraction). It was only after this contraction that God emitted beams of light into the resulting vacuum to bring about the world out of nothing. The first act of God, therefore, was not one of "revelation," but one of "self-limitation."

2. Shevirat Hakelim (The Breaking of the Vessels)—An Imperfect World

As the process of creation continued, divine light flowed into the primordial space. Certain vessels *(kelim)* assigned to shelter the upper three *sefirot* were able to absorb the light that entered into them. But, when the divine light reached the other seven *sefirot,* the vessels could not contain the power of the light and broke, with pieces shattering and falling away. Some of the light returned to its source; other divine "sparks" fell downward, some rose upward. This occurrence, called by Luria *shevirat hakelim* (the breaking of the vessels), caused a dramatic change in the universe. Everything was affected by this upheaval. As a result, nothing is in its proper place; it is either above or below. In other words, all beings are in exile *(galut)*.

3. Tikkun (Mending)—We Are Copartners with God

According to Luria, right after the original shattering of the vessels, God began to mend the world but left its completion to humanity. Had Adam not sinned in the Garden of Eden, the world would have entered into a messianic age at the time of creation. Adam's eating the fruit of the forbidden tree of knowledge, however, caused the breaking of the vessels again. This is why we live in an imperfect world. We are still in exile.

But there is hope. The world can be mended. We can repair the world. By bettering ourselves, we can fix the universe and return it to its original wholeness. This *tikkun* (mending) can be accomplished by observing the laws and commandments of the Torah. By doing *mitzvot,* we can free the imprisoned divine lights, raise them to their proper places, and restore the world *(tikkun olam)*.

Therefore, an individual who performs a *mitzvah* is not only doing the right thing but is also contributing to the mending of the entire universe. The future of the world is therefore in our hands. We are copartners with God in this divine and sacred task.

According to Luria, after we have fulfilled our duty and all things take their original places in the order of nature, redemption will come by itself. The Messiah will only symbolize the completion of the redemptive process.

Prayer Leads the Soul to God

In the Lurianic system, prayer plays a great role in the process of *tikkun*. Every *mitzvah* was to be accompanied by the recitation of a formula declaring that the act was done for the purpose of "uniting the Holy One, praised is He, and His *She-*

chinah, out of fear and love." Prayer is, therefore, more than the free expression of one's heart. It is a vehicle by which one's soul ascends to God. It is even more than this: Through prayer one can expect to influence the upper spheres of the universe, the domain of the Divine. *The Zohar* states:

> Whoever prays with tears before the Almighty can procure the cancellation of any chastisement that has been decreed against him.
> (*The Zohar,* I, 223a, vol. II, p. 316)

To do this, one needs to be able to concentrate fully on the act of prayer *(kavvanah).* The true worshiper, by means of a mystical prayer based on *kavvanah,* can cause changes, not only in his or her own inner world, but also in the spiritual world of the universe. This is, according to Luria, prayer at its best and the means to an intimate communion with God.

In Summary

The development of Judaism was influenced by a strong strain of mysticism, a belief that meditation and prayer can lead to communion with God. The early rabbis discouraged mystical speculation because of its potential for heresy. Still, a significant number of thinkers pursued mysticism.

For the mystics, God exists but is unknowable. Ten *sefirot,* emanating from God, gave shape to our physical world. We humans are a microcosm of the universe and unite the "upper" and the "lower" worlds.

Isaac Luria, a prominent mystic, postulated a self-limiting God who voluntarily contracted *(tzimtzum)* to make room for the physical world. In the aftermath of this contraction, certain divine vessels shattered *(shevirat hakelim),* scattering divine sparks throughout the world. Through performing *mitzvot* and through prayer, we humans can mend *(tikkun)* the world and bring it closer to perfection. In addition, our souls can approach the Divine.

6

THE PANTHEISM OF SPINOZA

Background

After the expulsion of the Jews from Spain in 1492, thousands of Jews dispersed throughout the world. Many of them first settled in Portugal and later made their way to Holland. Amsterdam became a center of Jewish life in northern Europe.

Baruch Spinoza was born in Amsterdam in 1632 to parents of Portuguese Jewish background. His father was a successful merchant. Like many other children, Spinoza was sent to the school of the local Jewish community where he excelled in his studies. In addition to studying the traditional Judaic subjects, he learned Latin and was able to read the classics of the Greco-Roman world.

Spinoza had a passion for philosophy and began to raise issues which the Jewish community considered to be heretical. He dared to question the Torah authorship of Moses. He wondered about whether or not Adam was really the first man. He asked how people could possibly believe that the law of Moses took precedence over natural law.

The Jewish scholarly community reacted with rage. In 1656, Spinoza was charged with heresy; he was excommunicated *(cherem)* and denied contact with other Jews. The decree,

signed by prominent members of the Jewish community of Amsterdam, stated that Spinoza had practiced "abominable heresies" and "monstrous acts." Spinoza accepted his excommunication with courage, saying, "It compels me to nothing which I should not have done in any case." Though treated as a pariah by the Jews, Spinoza did not join any other religious group. He lived alone, dedicating his life to philosophical pursuits, while making a meager living polishing eyeglass lenses.

Spinoza began to write down his ideas, though he was reluctant to publish them for fear of further harassment. When in 1670 his *Tractatus Theologico-Politicus* appeared unsigned, it was banned everywhere. Spinoza was offered important posts at institutes of higher learning under non-Jewish auspices, but he declined them, preferring a more private life. By 1674, he completed his major work entitled *Ethics Geometrically Demonstrated* (in short, *Ethics*), but he was unable to publish it. The only books that appeared in print during his lifetime were short essays and a book on the French philosopher Des-

cartes. He died of consumption in 1677. The books and letters
that made him famous appeared after his death.

Spinoza has been described as "the most impious atheist that
ever lived upon the face of the earth." On the other hand, he
has also been called a "God-intoxicated man." No one, however, can deny his influence on Western thought or his total
commitment to the pursuit of truth, and truth alone. "No man
has ever lived closer to what he himself taught."

There have been many attempts to revoke the edict of excommunication against Spinoza. At one point, Israeli Prime
Minister David Ben-Gurion urged that the *cherem* be lifted.
However, the religious leaders of Amsterdam (who are the
only group able to lift a ban initiated in their city) have not
responded favorably, perhaps because they believe that the
rabbinate today lacks the authority to void a decree of this
kind.

Spinoza's Search for Truth

In his all-consuming search for truth, Spinoza viewed mathematics as the most promising model for certain knowledge.
Influenced by Galileo's application of mathematics to the study
of nature, he sought to apply the same methodology to meta-
physics.

Spinoza drew upon both Jewish and non-Jewish sources in
developing his own philosophy. From the Spanish Kabbalists,
he learned of the oneness of the world and God. From Rabbi
Levi ben Gershon (Gersonides), he took the notion that the
universe is eternal. From Rabbi Chasdai Crescas, he gleaned
that the universe was the body of God. From non-Jewish thinkers, particularly the French philosopher Descartes (1596–
1650), he studied both the language of medieval philosophy
and important concepts that would help him formulate his
own thoughts.

Descartes argued that the world is made of two elements,

matter and mind. Spinoza, rejecting this dualism, maintained that mind and matter are two different forms of the same and only substance, neither one above the other. Therefore, spiritual and physical elements—God and the universe—are one and the same. This basic principle is the cornerstone of pantheism (from the Greek *pan* meaning "all" and *theos* meaning "God"), the philosophical view that all things share in the Divine.

The Nature of God

To explain the existence of matter in the world, Spinoza reasoned that matter had to come from God, the source of all things. Therefore, there must be only one substance, and that substance is God.

> Besides God no substance can be granted or conceived.*
>
> (*The Ethics*, I, 14, p. 54)

In other words:

> Whatsoever is, is in God, and without God nothing can be or be conceived.
>
> (Ibid., 15, p. 55)

Thus, for Spinoza, God is not the Creator of the universe; God and the universe are synonymous. The laws of nature were not established by God as an outside agent; they are the acts of God. There is an order in the universe, and everything functions according to this structure which existed in the past and will continue into the future. This obviously leads to a deterministic thinking, a sense that everything that

*All quotes are from *Chief Works of Benedict de Spinoza*, trans. R.H.M. Elwes; London: Bell, 1884.

happens in the world has been predetermined and cannot be influenced by human action. Spinoza argues that it cannot be otherwise.

> Things could not have been brought into being by God in any other manner or in any order different from that which has in fact obtained.
>
> (Ibid., 33, p. 70)

In this statement, we should not be misled by the words "brought into being by God." Spinoza does not believe that God acts from the outside of nature. Quite the contrary, as we can see from another statement.

> All things are conditioned by the necessity of the divine nature.
>
> (Ibid., 29, p. 68)

Whereas other thinkers maintain that God acts independently of the world and uses will and power to affect our lives, Spinoza says that the "will of God" is none other than the workings of nature. Therefore, all events are the mechanical operation of natural-divine laws which function according to their predetermined pattern.

God, according to Spinoza, is not a personal God. God does not have an intellect or will, does not watch over us, does not know us, is not a loving Parent. God simply is revealed through the laws of nature. To assume that God acts one way toward some people and differently towards others is to claim that God can be limited by external environment, and that in Spinoza's view is nonsense. God, he says, is perfect—lacks nothing, never changes, and is in fact the totality of everything in existence.

Good and Evil

If our world is a world of determinism and not of design, and if God acts according to a set pattern, what, then, is the meaning of good and evil? More importantly, does one truly have a choice in how to act? Moralists have maintained that God has provided human beings with two alternatives, either to follow the path of good or the path of evil. In any case, the choice is ours. Spinoza's assertion that everything is predetermined makes moral choice impossible if not absurd.

Spinoza argued that God is beyond good and evil. In fact, the terms "good" and "bad" are relative to human experience and have no universal validity outside of ourselves. He writes:

> As for the terms good and bad, they indicate no positive quality in things regarded in themselves but are merely modes of thinking, or notions which we form from the comparison of things one with another. Thus one and the same thing can be at the same time good, bad, and indifferent. For instance, music is good for him that is melancholy, bad for him that mourns; for him that is deaf, it is neither good nor bad.
>
> (*The Ethics*, IV, pre., p. 189)

In fact, Spinoza maintained, to claim that we have freedom of choice is an illusion. We are not free to do what we want. Everything we do is conditioned by circumstances that precede them, and these circumstances are determined by causes that precede them as well, and so on. We are only free when we have knowledge.

> Whenever, then, anything in nature seems to us ridiculous, absurd, or evil, it is because we have but a partial knowledge of things and are in the main igno-

rant of the order and coherence of nature as a whole, and because we want everything to be arranged according to the dictates of our own reason.

(A Political Treatise, II, 8, p. 295)

For Spinoza, to "know God" means to understand, as much as we are capable, the relationship between parts of the world. In particular, it means to know our place in the universe.

The fact that we realize that our will is not free does not mean that we are not responsible for our behavior. On the contrary, Spinoza argued that determinism makes for a better moral life. It teaches us not to despise any one; we are more likely to forgive evil people because in a sense they did not know what they were doing. And even if we have to punish wicked people in society for the sake of preserving a social order, we do it without hate. On the other hand, determinism forces us to welcome everything in life with an accepting mind. We realize that events follow by necessity from the eternal decrees of God. And God is not a capricious being who curses one and blesses another. No one should or could blame God for all the evils of the universe, for God did not actually "cause" them to affect individual beings. If anything, God is the sustainer of the order of the universe for all times.

This philosophy, some argue, leads to resignation. We take the world as it is, without complaint. We say yes to life as to death. We learn to deal with our own limitations and try to preserve ourselves as best we can.

Immortality

Spinoza maintained that, as anything else in the universe, we humans, too, are part of the great stream of law and order of the universe that is God.

The greatest good is the knowledge of the union which the mind has with the whole of nature.
(On the Improvement of the Intellect)

We are, therefore, immortal. The human mind remains forever.

The human mind cannot be absolutely destroyed with the body, but there remains of it something which is eternal.
(The Ethics, V, 23, p. 259)

This does not mean that Spinoza believes in heavenly reward. In fact, he writes that "blessedness is not the reward of virtue, but virtue itself." Similarly, as one commentator noted, for Spinoza immortality is not the reward of clear thinking but clear thought itself.

In Summary

One of the greatest pantheists of all time, Baruch Spinoza argued that God and the universe are of one and the same substance. Free will is a human illusion. In reality, everything flows by necessity from the order of the universe. Determinism teaches us to take the world as it is. We are at peace with ourselves when we know our place in the universe and accept it. Our goal is to know God. "The mind's highest good is the knowledge of God and the mind's highest virtue is to know God" *(The Ethics,* IV, 28, p. 205).

7

THE PHILOSOPHY OF

DIALOGUE OF BUBER

Background

Martin Buber, one of the most influential Jewish thinkers of
our time, was born in Vienna in 1878. He spent his childhood
in Lemberg, Galicia, with his grandfather, Solomon Buber, the
noted midrashic scholar. From him he learned not only rabbin-
ics but also an appreciation of the writings of the chasidic
masters.

Buber received his secular education at the universities of
Vienna, Leipzig, Zurich, and Berlin. He began his writing career as a cultural Zionist interested in the development
of educational youth programs. In 1901, he became the editor of the Zionist periodical, *Die Welt.* After the First
World War, he became involved in various cultural activities and, in fact, emerged as the key proponent of what
he called "Hebrew humanism," which promoted, among
other things, Jewish-Arab cooperation and coexistence in
Palestine.

Buber's active public life, however, did not stand in the
way of his philosophical and scholarly pursuits. In 1923, he

published a book, *Ich und Du* (I and Thou), which contains his philosophy of dialogue. Two years later, he and his colleague, Franz Rosenzweig, began to create a new Bible translation.

In 1938, Buber escaped from Nazi Germany and settled in Palestine. He was appointed professor of social philosophy at the Hebrew University in Jerusalem and taught there until his retirement in 1951. In Israel, Buber founded a number of cultural institutions and was voted the first president of the Israel Academy of Sciences and Humanities (1960–62). Following the Second World War, and until his death in 1965, he traveled extensively all over the world, influencing both Jews and Christians with his unique approach to the problems of the world and society.

Buber wrote many books and essays on chasidism, Zionism, and philosophy. Among his major works are *I and Thou, Between Man and Man,* and *Eclipse of God.*

Real Meeting

One of Buber's major concerns was how to discover true reality. Because of the limits of human perception, we are often misled by appearances. But what is the "thing" in itself? For example, when we look at a person and observe his or her bodily features, we take note of eye color, the shape of the face, contours of body. But who is the "real person," the identity behind our perception? This we often fail to capture. Following the German philosopher Kant, Buber argued that we cannot know any object or person "in itself" apart from its relation to us. In Buber's view, perfect knowledge can only be obtained by means of a dialogue, possible only through a real encounter. This constitutes the basic imperative of life.

All real living is meeting.
(*I and Thou,* p. 11; Scribner's, 1958)

Two Types of Meeting

How do we establish a dialogue with others? Buber says that we relate to others in two distinct ways. One is "I-It" and the other "I-Thou."

1. "I-It"
This relationship is one of "experiencing and using." The person (in this case, "I") who "uses" the other to satisfy personal needs relates to the other as an object, an "It." For example, when a cab driver takes a passenger to a designated place and gets paid for that service, the relationship between the two is one of "use." Each is "using" the other for personal benefit. Similarly, the relationship between a buyer and a

seller, or a writer and an editor, falls essentially within the realm of an "I-It." These relationships often lack "mutuality." There is no real concern or true acceptance of the other person. These people are simply providing services for one another. When we enter into an "I-It" relationship, we pass judgment, we evaluate, we "use."

An "I-It" relationship is not necessarily bad. In fact, most of our contacts take place within the framework of an "I-It." At times, we relate on an "I-It" basis, not only to strangers, but also to the members of our immediate family, as when I ask my son to bring me a glass of water, or when I hurriedly help my daughter with her homework, or when I take the dog out for a walk.

2. "I-Thou"

"I and Thou" does not mean exclusively "I and God." It refers to an intimate relationship between the subject ("I") and any other being or thing, including God.

Buber speaks of "I-Thou" as a higher relationship than "I-It," one in which the two parties fully accept one another. One does not "use" the other; one does not judge the other. In this real encounter, there is mutual confirmation of their separate selves. It is as if the two have the capacity to feel each other's pains and joys.

In this mutual relationship of "I-Thou," the subject does not lose its identity. In other words, the "I" does not become one with the "Thou." Buber, who is no mystic, does not claim that in an "I-Thou" meeting the two parties reach a total communion. On the contrary, each one retains his/her individuality, remains separate from the other, and, yet, completely accepts and confirms the other.

This "I-Thou" relationship, adds Buber, does not continue forever. The moment we become aware of the nature of the encounter, the element of judgment interferes and "the contact" turns into an "I-It."

Every Thou in the world is by its nature fated to become a thing.

(Ibid., p. 17)

What had been a genuine relationship becomes a mere "experience." This transformation is normal, for otherwise, for example, a physician would become indistinguishable from his/her patient.

In Buber's system, the sphere of relationship is not limited to human beings but may include animals, trees, objects of nature, and God. In other words, just as we establish an "I-Thou" relationship with another person, so can we relate to a rock, a tree, a flower, or a pet, even though in these cases the relation is not fully reciprocal. Buber himself relates that at age eleven he had an "I-Thou" relationship with his horse.

> When I was eleven years of age, spending the summer on my grandparents' estate, I used . . . to steal into the stable and gently stroke the neck of my darling, a broad dapple-grey horse. . . . When I stroked the mighty mane . . . and felt the life beneath my hand, it was as though the element of vitality itself bordered on my skin. . . . It let me approach, confided itself to me, placed itself elementally in the real relation of Thou and Thou with me. The horse, even when I had not begun by pouring oats for him in the manger, very gently raised his massive head, ears flicking, then snorted quietly, as a conspirator gives a signal to be recognizable only by his fellow-conspirator; and I was approved.
>
> (*Between Man and Man,* p. 23; Macmillan, 1965)

God—The "Eternal Thou"

Buber argued that, even though the "I-Thou" relationship is by necessity a passing one, there is a "Thou" which, because of its nature, can never become an "It." God, in the words of Buber, is the "Eternal Thou." God is ever present, while we at times are absent. Whenever we enter into a genuine relationship with another, we also discover God.

In Buber's way of thinking, it is not possible to define God or to prove God's existence, for God is not an object, an "It," capable of being measured by the yardsticks of our human mind.

> By the term "God" I mean not a metaphysical idea, nor a moral idea, nor a projection of a psychic or social image, nor anything at all created by, or developed within, man.
>
> (*On Judaism*, p. 4; Schocken, 1972)

People have always tried to create images of God. However, these ideas represent only our attempt to grasp the inexplicable when we encounter God. God cannot be defined, described, or proven. God can only be "met."

We do not have to abandon our daily activities in order to encounter the Divine. True to his chasidic background, Buber taught that we can meet God in the ordinary activities of daily life, if only we enter into a genuine dialogue with others. In this spirit, he told the following story.

The Rabbi of Kotzk once asked: "Where is the dwelling place of God?" His learned students laughed. "What a thing to ask! Is not the whole world full of God's glory?" The rabbi answered his own question: "God dwells wherever a person lets God in!"

Every time we have an "I-Thou" relationship, Buber said, we also have an encounter with the "Eternal Thou" who is God.

In each Thou we address the Eternal Thou.
(I and Thou, p. 101)

Every particular Thou is a glimpse through to the Eternal Thou; by means of every particular Thou the primary word addresses the Eternal Thou.

(Ibid., p. 75)

Every true relationship, therefore, is also a dialogue with God. To meet God, as our "Eternal Thou," we must give up our instinct for detachment and try to enter the world of relationship with all our being.

The Result of the Meeting

To try to explain the details of the real encounter between the "I" and the "Thou" is fruitless, for every such description invites judgment and evaluation by our minds, thereby turning the "Thou" into an "It." It is like describing the experience of being in love. If you have never been in love, no description will explain it adequately. If you have been fortunate to know love, there is no need for an additional explanation. Nevertheless, the "I-Thou" encounter is not without its results.

Through the "Thou" a man becomes "I."

(Ibid., p. 28)

As a result of this meeting, a person becomes more sensitive, more responsive, more human. Also, a person receives a revelation. This revelation is simply a realization that the individual has been in the living presence of another and, ultimately, of God. In other words, the encounter does not result in the transmission of a particular message.

Man receives, and he receives not a specific "content" but a Presence, a Presence as power.

(Ibid., p. 110)

There is a personal enrichment as a result of a genuine meeting. We return to our work with greater insight, with deeper sensitivity, though not with a specific "how to." Each one of us reacts according to our personal understanding.

All revelation is summons and sending.

(Ibid., p. 115)

The Revelation of Torah

Buber denied that the giving of the Torah at Sinai contained a one-time revelation of laws.

Creation is the origin, redemption the goal. But revelation is not a fixed, dated point poised between the two. The revelation at Sinai is not this midpoint itself, but the perceiving of it, and such perception is possible at any time.

("The Man of Today and the Jewish Bible," *On the Bible*, p. 6; Schocken, 1968)

For Buber, the Sinai event did not produce moral and cultic prescriptions of eternal and universal validity. Laws and statutes can only be accepted as the embodiment of a real address by God to particular individuals. This view by necessity leads to ethical relativism, namely, what is right for you may be wrong for me.

The rejection of the validity and authoritative nature of Jewish law brought Buber in conflict with many of his contemporaries, including Franz Rosenzweig. Like Buber, Rosenzweig argued that revelation does not yield knowledge of God's essence. In his book *The Star of Redemption*, he wrote:

All that God ever reveals in revelation is revelation. . . . He reveals nothing but himself to man.

But Rosenzweig maintained that the Torah, as the product of an encounter between the Jewish people and God, obligated us to keep the Torah and live by it. In fact, he added, all Jews must raise the "legislations" in the Torah to the level of "commandments" as though they had been directly addressed to them. Buber denied that Jews were duty bound to practice the Torah simply because it was revealed in the past. Nothing, he believed, should interfere with the dialogue between the "I" and the "Thou," as understood by the "I."

The Problem of Evil

Buber's thinking on the difficult subject of evil changed over time. In his early years, Buber dealt with evil as part of his general philosophy of dialogue. He argued that the failure to enter into a genuine dialogue constitutes evil. On the other hand, reestablishing the dialogue leads to the redemption, or overcoming, of evil. For Buber, an "I-It" relationship in and of itself is not evil, only an exclusively "I-It" orientation is evil.

> The primary word I-It is not evil—as matter is not evil. . . . If a man lets it have the mastery, the continually growing world of *It* overruns him and robs him of the reality of his own I.
>
> (*I and Thou*, p. 46)

Buber identified two stages of evil: The first stage is characterized by a lack of decision, a lack of direction. Instead of acting, we remain passive. We do not exercise our freedom to act, but instead merely let things happen. The second stage is the actual decision to *do* evil. In Buber's thinking, therefore, human nature is not evil, what is evil is the misuse of freedom.

Later in life, and primarily as a response to the Holocaust, Buber advanced the notion of "radical evil." There are some extraordinary times, said Buber, when God withdraws from humanity. In the words of the Bible, God, as it were, "hides His face" (Job. 13:24; cf. Isa. 8:17, 45:15). We do not always know the meaning of this "eclipse of God," the "silence of God," the loss of God's nearness. Buber does not provide us with an explanation of this "radical evil," but only with a question emerging from a broken heart: Can we believe in a God who allowed these terrible things to happen, enter into a genuine dialogue with this God, and, like Job, "hear" God's voice? Buber leaves this latter question unanswered.

In Summary

Martin Buber introduced a new way of thinking and relating to others. In doing so, he exposed one of our human weaknesses, namely our treating others as objects, "using" them as things or relating to them for personal benefit. In his terminology, we turn them into an "It." As long as we concentrate only on our own selves, we may be able to gain comfort and prosperity in life but will never be able to become genuine human beings. That is only possible through an "I-Thou" relationship which elevates us to a higher plane of existence. "The relation with man is the real simile of the relation with God; in it true address receives true response" (*I and Thou*, p. 103).

It is by genuinely relating to others as "Thou" that we meet our "Eternal Thou," God. This is not done by denying the world and our work in it. On the contrary, it is within the context of how everyday life is lived that God is truly revealed.

8

THE LIMITED THEISM

OF STEINBERG

Background:
Basic Concepts of Classical Theism

Many people assume that those who believe in God are called "theists" and those who do not are known as "atheists." In reality, theism (from the Greek, *theos,* meaning "God") is one among many different concepts of God. It is not the only one, though it may be the most popular.

Classical theists, in the main, believe that:

1. God is one and alone; there are no other gods beside the one and only God.
2. God, though not possessing a body, is a spiritual Being who expresses will, love, and concern for the created world.
3. God is all-powerful; that is, God is capable of upsetting the laws of nature at will. In other words, God can create miracles.
4. God is all-good.
5. God is all-knowing; God "knows" what happened in the past and what will happen in the future.
6. God is supernatural and transnatural; in other words, God is outside of, as well as within, the universe.

7. God "knows" us, "hears" our prayers and "answers" them, though we may not always realize how or when.

We saw Jewish theism expressed most clearly in the biblical and rabbinic periods (chapters 1 and 2).

Proofs for the Existence of God

Throughout the centuries, many philosophers, including a number of Jewish thinkers we have already discussed, advanced arguments "proving" the existence of God. To review:

1. The ontological (from the Greek *ontos* meaning, "being," "existence") argument derives God's existence from the idea of God, claiming that the very idea of perfection which characterizes God implies God's existence.

2. The teleological (from the Greek, *telos,* meaning "purpose," "design") argument is based on the observation that

there is order in the universe, and this order implies the existence of an organizing Mind. We saw this "proof" articulated by Philo.

3. The cosmological argument, advanced by Maimonides, indicates that there must be a beginning to the process of motion; that is, One that started the motion without being moved.

4. There is a moral argument which points to God as the source of all our moral decisions.

Other philosophers and religious thinkers have added arguments derived from historical events, mystical experiences, and divine revelation as reflected in nature and in the Holy Scriptures.

The Problem of Evil

Classical theism insists that God is both all-powerful and all-good. If this is so, then why is there evil in the world? Classical theists, who believe that God is the source of good and evil, advance various explanations. Some maintain that evil is the result of a prior sin; others argue that evil is only the absence of good. There are those who say that evil is temporary, and, therefore, those who suffer in this world will be rewarded in the world-to-come. (See chapter 2, p. 37.) Some simply state that evil is an enigma which cannot be resolved by the human mind.

On the other hand, some thinkers have found a possible answer in the notion that God's powers are limited. This position is usually known as "limited theism." There have been many thinkers, both Jewish and non-Jewish, who have defended this line of reasoning. One of the most articulate Jewish advocates of this view was Rabbi Milton Steinberg.

Biographical Background

Milton Steinberg was born in Rochester, New York, in 1903. He studied at City College in New York City where he was influenced by his professor of philosophy, Morris R. Cohen. In 1923, he entered the Jewish Theological Seminary (Conservative) and was ordained a rabbi in 1928. While at the seminary he identified with the teachings of the founder of Reconstructionism, Rabbi Mordecai M. Kaplan, and after his ordination remained one of Kaplan's disciples. However, he did not join the movement and, at times, even raised a number of criticisms of Kaplan's thinking. After serving his first congregation in Indianapolis, he returned to New York in 1933 to become the rabbi of the Park Avenue Synagogue. He held that position until his death in 1950, at the age of forty-seven.

During his short but brilliant career, Steinberg wrote extensively on the nature of God, the question of faith in the modern world, and the impact of non-Jewish thought on contemporary Jewish philosophy. He was also active in Zionist circles and lectured on Jewish and Zionist issues. His first book, *The Making of the Modern Jew*, dealt with the history of the Jews from the time of the Second Temple to the establishment of the State of Israel. In *A Partisan Guide to the Jewish Problem*, Steinberg discussed the kind of Jew who would emerge in the modern world. His historical novel, *As a Driven Leaf*, used the Talmud as background for discussing important theological problems of the day. *Basic Judaism* enjoyed—and continues to enjoy—tremendous popularity. It is a classic text which sets down the fundamentals of Judaism in clear language, explaining Judaism from both a traditional and a liberal perspective.

Two of Steinberg's books appeared after his death: *A Believing Jew* and *Anatomy of Faith*. Both deal with important theological questions. In addition to these volumes, Steinberg wrote numerous articles, essays, and sermons, some of which were published in book form.

Starting with Faith

Like many other thinkers, Steinberg starts with the idea that human knowledge about God is necessarily limited by our own human shortcomings.

> We cannot know God completely. At the essence of God—what He is in himself—we can only guess; and of His manifestations or works we comprehend only that shred which our senses can grasp and our mind conceive.
>
> (*Basic Judaism,* pp. 39–40; Harcourt, 1947)

He argues that we must accept the existence of God on faith alone. Logic by itself cannot bring us to the belief in God.

> For like all other propositions, that of the existence of God is not completely provable. It remains the conclusion of an act of faith.
>
> (*Anatomy of Faith,* p. 74; Harcourt, 1960)

A religious interpretation of reality, argues Steinberg, makes more sense. It may not be as certain as a scientific theory, but for that matter even science is based on certain assumptions which are taken for granted.

> Here before me unfolds a universe which is dynamic, creative, and rational in the sense that everything in it conforms to the law of its own being, a world that has produced in living things what seems to be purposiveness and in man the phenomenon of consciousness. No other theory except that which posits a Thought-Will as the essence of things fits such a scene.
>
> (*A Believing Jew,* p. 21; Harcourt, 1951)

Steinberg's Understanding of God

Steinberg does not provide us with a short definition of what he means by God, though he views God in theistic terms.

> The entire universe, as I see it, is the outward manifestation of Mind-Energy, of Spirit, or to use the older and better word, of God. God is then the essential Being of all beings, though all beings in their totality do not exhaust Him.
>
> (Ibid., p. 19)

Steinberg maintains that God is not only a Power but also a Mind, akin to our own. God is purposive and ethical. God enters into relations with the created world and primarily with humankind. Yet, Steinberg readily admits, God is not all-powerful. He comes to this conclusion in order to allow human freedom on the one hand and the presence of evil on the other.

> God is Absolute in the sense of being a Creator to whom we stand as creatures while being at the same time a self-limiting Power. To the extent of the reality of our freedom, God is limited in His power. . . . If a man is to have real freedom, God's control cannot be complete.
>
> (*Anatomy of Faith,* pp. 273-4)

The belief in the all-powerful nature of God creates a major problem for Steinberg. He clearly states:

> God is indubitably the power of rationality, of design, of order, of meaningfulness, of creativity; yet traditional conceptions of God . . . are somehow inadequate to deal with the problem of evil.
>
> (Ibid.)

How Do We Explain Evil

Limited theists, Steinberg included, argue that nature is in the process of evolving according to God's will to higher and better levels. However, in each species of the universe there are some lower levels of development. Evil is to be found in these lower stages.

> [Evil] represents the survival into the human condition of other, lower stages of reality, mineral, vegetable, and animal, out of which man has emerged, or on which he stands.
>
> (*Basic Judaism*, p. 55)

> It is the persistence of the circumstances of lower strata in higher; the carry-over of the limitations of the orders of being on which man's existence is based into his personality and society.
>
> (*A Believing Jew*, p. 26)

Or, said another way:

> It is the still unremoved scaffolding of the edifice of God's creativity.
>
> (Ibid., p. 28)

The advantage of recognizing the reality of evil as part of the makeup of the universe, and particularly as part of nature which has not as yet been conquered, enables us not to assign blame to God.

> The concept of irrational evil prevents us from ascribing to God that which probably should not be ascribed to Him. God is exempted, not from the struggle, but from the responsibility for the elements of chance within His universe.
>
> (*Anatomy of Faith*, p. 275)

Thus, for example, if there is a tragedy, we do not say that it was brought about by God but that it happened because of the lower levels of development within the universe.

God: Not All-Powerful but All-Good

How does one relate to a God who is not all-powerful but all-good? One thinker, Rabbi Levi Olan, a Reform rabbi who espoused a belief in limited theism, states that it is all a matter of language and symbols. At one time, he argues, people thought of God as a king who could do anything. God, furthermore, was not a mortal king, but a King of kings, and as such all-powerful. This image is now irrelevant. We would be better served in our time, Olan adds, by the old Jewish idea of God as father:

> A father is both inside the child and outside of him. He is, if you will, immanent and transcendent at one and the same time. In our childhood, father was all-knowing, all-powerful; he could do everything. As we mature the image changes; father no longer knows everything and cannot do everything. Yet, he is probably closer and nearer to us. . . . Analogies are always difficult. . . . Yet, if pictorialize we must, the figure of a father who loves us and cannot always do what he would love to do for us comes closer to our experience than that of an absolute monarch.
>
> ("An Organicist View," *The Theological Foundations of Prayer,* p. 60; Union of American Hebrew Congregations, 1967)

Humanity as God's Co-worker

Given the fact that nature contains certain aspects which are less than perfect and, as such, becomes the source of evil in the world, limited theists have advocated that humanity has a major role to play in overcoming these limitations. In this endeavor, they stated, God needs the help of humankind and we need the help of God. As Steinberg expresses it:

> Both He and His creation are then faced with a common task and a common battle. They may share together in opposing the same unreason and bringing greater light and order in the universe.
> *(Anatomy of Faith*, p. 275)

In Summary

Limited theism is based on the assumption that God is all-good but not all-powerful. This explains the existence of evil. Milton Steinberg, a Conservative rabbi who espoused this philosophy, argued that a religious interpretation of the universe makes more sense, even though it is impossible to prove with absolute certainty that God exists. This belief is a matter of faith which, like any other hypothesis, must pass the test of plausibility, practicality, and simplicity. God, Steinberg added, is not all-powerful; otherwise it would be impossible to maintain human freedom. Furthermore, the presence of evil also shows that there are things which God cannot do, as a result of God's self-limitation. Evil, "the still unremoved scaffolding of the edifice of God's creativity," is a challenge to God and humanity, in that it calls both to join hands for the purpose of eliminating its vestiges. Thus, we become partners with God in the work of creation and in the realization of the cosmic design.

9

THE RELIGIOUS NATURALISM

OF KAPLAN

Background

Mordecai M. Kaplan, author, educator, and founder of the Reconstructionist movement, had a profound influence on the development of American Jewish life. His ideas brought about Reconstructionism, a fourth branch of American Judaism (joining Reform, Orthodox, and Conservative), and also such innovations as the *bat mitzvah,* the Jewish community center, and the *chavurah.*

Born in 1881, Kaplan immigrated from Lithuania to the United States at the age of nine. He studied at City College of New York and Columbia University then entered the rabbinic program of the Jewish Theological Seminary (Conservative). There he received his ordination in 1902. He served briefly as rabbi of an Orthodox congregation in New York, leaving to become dean of the newly founded Teachers' Institute of the seminary. After retiring in 1963, Kaplan taught at the Hebrew University in Jerusalem. He returned to the United States shortly before his death in 1983, at the age of 102.

Kaplan's interest in Jewish community organization began in the early years of his seminary career. In 1918, he set up the

first Jewish center in New York City, hoping to bring together Jews of various backgrounds for religious as well as cultural activities. Kaplan is also credited with the idea of establishing summer camps for the education and recreation of Jewish youth. In 1922, Kaplan founded the Society for the Advancement of Judaism, which later became the Jewish Reconstructionist Foundation (1935). It was through his efforts that the Reconstructionist Rabbinical College was established in Philadelphia, Pennsylvania, in 1968, an institution which has since ordained both male and female rabbis. The Reconstructionist movement today has a rabbinic association as well as an organization of affiliated congregations, The Reconstructionist Federation of Congregations and Havurot.

An early champion of women's rights in Judaism, Kaplan created the *bat mitzvah* ceremony, with his daughter, Judith, becoming the first *bat mitzvah* in 1922.

Kaplan wrote many books and articles articulating his religious philosophy. Among his major works are *Judaism as a Civilization, Judaism without Supernaturalism, The Meaning of God in Modern Jewish Religion,* and *Questions Jews Ask.*

Judaism as a Civilization

"Civilization" is a key term in Reconstructionism. Kaplan defined Judaism as "the evolving religious civilization of the Jewish people." He divided Jewish history into four major periods: biblical, rabbinic, modern (1800–1948), and contemporary (from the end of the Second World War to the present time)—each with its own requirements for Jewish advancement:

> The conditions which enabled Judaism to flourish in the past are irrevocably gone with the wind. Nothing less than original and creative thinking in terms of present-day realities and future responsibilities can create anew the conditions which are indispensable to Jewish survival.
>
> *(The Reconstructionist,* 8, 1942)

Many Jews, he noted, no longer believe in divine revelation or miracles. Furthermore, the social, cultural, and political conditions of contemporary America differ from those of Europe. Therefore:

> The indispensable requisite to Jewish survival is Jewish revival—revival in all phases of Jewish life: structural, religious, moral, and cultural.
>
> (Ibid.)

Reconstructionism proposed to shift the center of gravity from the Jewish religion to the Jewish people.

Judaism existed for the Jewish people, and not the
Jewish people for Judaism.

(Ibid.)

Kaplan did not believe that the Jewish people had superseded religion. He maintained that the preservation of our
religion required that Jews also identify with the other aspects
of their ancient civilization—history, literature, language, social organizations, folk customs, standards of culture, social and
spiritual ideals, and esthetic values. Kaplan viewed Zion as the
spiritual center of this rich civilization. Outside of Israel, he
asserted, Judaism functions as a secondary civilization for most
Jews.

Kaplan's Naturalism

Kaplan's naturalistic God concept is based on the proposition
that the world can be explained in terms of scientifically verifi-
able ideas.

People in the past, Kaplan tells us, related to God as if God
were a source of magical powers that responded to human
wishes. Most believers considered God a supernatural Being
who operated in the world, unbound by the limitations of
natural law. Unfortunately, adds Kaplan, some people still
think in this way.

To most people God is not really God but a magnified
demon. That is why they cannot disassociate religion
from supernaturalism.

(*Without Supernaturalism,* p. 39; Jewish
Reconstructionist Press, 1958)

In our time, however, people with a certain level of scientific
sophistication cannot consider religion as entering into a relationship with the supernatural.

What kind of religion does a modern person need? Kaplan's answer is clear:

> The only kind of religion that can help him live and get the most out of life will be the one which will teach him to identify as divine or holy whatever in human nature or in the world about him enhances human life.
>
> (*Meaning,* p. 25; Jewish Reconstructionist Press, 1962)

God: A Power
That Makes for Human Salvation

All human beings, wrote Kaplan, have physical as well as spiritual needs.

> Man, once his physiological needs are satisfied, begins to experience the need to overcome such traits as self-indulgence, arrogance, envy, exploitation, and hatred, or to bring under control the aggressive forces of his nature.
>
> (*Questions,* p. 83; Jewish Reconstructionist Press, 1956)

Yet, if it is true that we have these higher needs (and religion encourages us to rise above our natural instincts), there must be something in the universe which helps us to achieve them.

> The cosmos is so constituted as to enable man to fulfill this highest human need of his nature.
>
> (Ibid.)

We believe intuitively that the universe operates in the direction of encouraging human growth and development. Life is meaningful and functions as the source of ethical and spiritual values. The idea of God is connected with this assumption which, like any intuitively-based assumption, requires no proof.

> Man normally veers in the direction of that which makes for the fulfillment of his destiny as a human being. That fact indicates the functioning of a cosmic Power which influences his behavior.
>
> (Ibid., p. 84)

Kaplan defined his concept of God in a variety of ways in various places. For example, God is:

> The sum of everything in the world that renders life significant and worthwhile—or holy.

> The totality of those forces in life that render human life worthwhile.

> The Power that impels man to become fully human.

> The sum of the animating, organizing forces and relationships which are forever making a cosmos out of chaos.

> The Power that makes for the fulfillment of all valid ideals.

In brief:

> God is the Power that makes for salvation.
> (*Meaning*, p. 40; see also *Without Supernaturalism*,
> pp. 114–115)

Meaning of "Salvation"

How does Kaplan define "salvation"? In rabbinic Judaism, as we have seen, salvation was something that took place in the world-to-come. It was there that the sufferer would be rewarded and the wicked punished. Yet, as Kaplan points out:

> The conduct of people today is motivated not by the desire to win for themselves a "share in the world-to-come," which would reward all their earthly efforts and compensate all their earthly suffering, but by the desire to win for themselves a share in this world, to win success, honor, love, and everything that contributes to human well-being and self-fulfillment on earth.
>
> (*Meaning*, p. 44)

Given this expectation, a new definition of salvation is needed that will satisfy the modern person. Kaplan, therefore, identified salvation with "self-realization" or "self-fulfillment."

> Self-fulfillment or self-realization is nothing more than the modern equivalent of what in general life is expressed by the term "salvation" and in traditional Jewish life by the phrase "having a share in the world-to-come."
>
> (Ibid., p. 41)

Though we cannot think of salvation in the way our ancestors did, it is still an indispensable element of our religious perspective. No individual is a self-sufficient entity. Every person yearns to become the best that he or she can be.

Belief in God

Kaplan assumed that there are reliable forces and processes in life that can contribute to self-improvement. Belief in God is an affirmation of this assumption. When we believe in God, Kaplan wrote, "we believe that reality . . . is so constituted as to enable man to achieve salvation" (*ibid.*, p. 26).

In other words:

> To believe in God means to take for granted that it is man's destiny to rise above the brute and to eliminate all forms of violence and exploitation from human society.
>
> (*Without Supernaturalism*, p. 112)

Our belief constitutes for us a program of action. For, as Kaplan points out:

> It matters very little how we conceive God, as long as we so believe in God that belief in Him makes a tremendous difference in our lives.
>
> (*Questions*, p. 87)

If God is, as Kaplan argued, that Power which makes for truth, for good, for justice, for freedom, then whenever we display moral responsibility we manifest the presence of God. To the extent that we strive to know the moral law and live up to it, we achieve, in Kaplan's words, "salvation" or "self-realization."

Is God a Power or a Person?

In the Middle Ages, noted Kaplan, people thought of God as "pure soul," without a body, yet possessing human traits. Modern scientists reject the dichotomy between body and soul or between matter and spirit. Today we think in terms of energy passing from one stage to another.

> We cannot conceive of God any more as a sort of invisible superman, displaying the same psychological traits as man, but on a greater scale. We cannot think of Him as loving, pitying, rewarding, punishing. . . .
>
> *(Meaning,* p. 88)

Kaplan prefers to speak of God, not as a person, but as the Power or the Process. We cannot think of God, adds Kaplan, as if God were "a concretized substance." In other words, we cannot "thingify Godhood."

> God is the Process by which the universe produces persons, and persons are the process by which God is manifest in the individual.
>
> *(Questions,* p. 103)

Does that mean that we should give up the idea of a "personal God"? No, says Kaplan:

> A God who makes a difference in one's personal life should be designated as a personal God.
>
> (Ibid., p. 104)

Kaplan's God is not synonymous with the universe but with that aspect of the universe which brings human fulfillment. In other words, Kaplan is not a pantheist. (See chapter 6, "The Pantheism of Spinoza.")

Are Miracles Possible?

The concept of God advanced by Kaplan does not allow for miracles, the suspension of natural law.

So long as men turn to God as though He were a personified cosmic dynamo, religion partakes of magic.

(*Without Supernaturalism*, p. 100)

Our belief in God must be consistent with our knowledge of the universe.

We cannot, for example, believe that God performs miracles and, at the same time, believe in the uniformities of natural law demanded by scientific theory.

(*Meaning*, p. 20)

Can we, then, afford to ignore our tradition which affirms such miracles? The answer is, again, no.

That tradition records the gropings and searchings which went on in the consciousness of our ancestors. Would we want to forget our own childish notions? . . . If we study the tradition carefully, we are bound to discover nuances and anticipations of attitudes toward life that were not only tenable but well worth cultivating. Those are the permanent values in our tradition, which we cannot afford to ignore.

(*Without Supernaturalism*, p. 112)

The Meaning of Prayer

If God is a Process, and not a person, what is the meaning of prayer for Kaplan? Can a Process "hear" our prayers?

In Kaplan's system, prayer takes on a different meaning. We do not pray "to" a Process, he says. We only call our attention to the Process.

Prayer aims at deriving, from the Process that constitutes God, the power that would strengthen the forces and relationships by which we fulfill ourselves as persons.

> (*Questions,* p. 103)

For Kaplan, a religious prayer is:

The utterance of those thoughts that imply either the actual awareness of God, or the desire to attain such awareness.

> (*Meaning,* p. 33)

The key word in this statement is "utterance." It is not important if our prayers are actually "heard." It is more significant if a person "voices" his or her yearnings for the achievement of all the goals which in their totality spell God. In other words, by expressing our hopes, aspirations, and desires for those aspects of life which are most worthwhile, we also take the first step toward their realization. Our expression becomes our goal, our wishes and yearnings, our program.

When we address ourselves to God in a prayer of petition, we raise to the level of consciousness those desires, the fulfillment of which we regard as a prerequisite to the fulfillment of our human destiny.

> (*Questions,* p. 85)

Obviously, prayer, understood from Kaplan's perspective, can only be effective on ourselves and not on the world outside. Prayer changes those who pray, giving them that courage and hope which they need to achieve the goals expressed in the prayer itself. Consequently, we should not expect prayers alone to alter natural events or conditions.

The Problem of Evil

How does Kaplan deal with the problem of evil? As we noted before, Kaplan identifies God with those aspects of the universe which enhance human life. The opposite is true of evil. In other words, evil is that aspect of life which hinders self-realization. Even more so, evil is that part of the universe which God has not as yet subdued.

> [It is] chaos still uninvaded by the creative energy, sheer chance unconquered by will and intelligence.
> *(Meaning,* pp. 72–73)

The growing capacity of people and science to eliminate or transform evil in the world, whether war, disease, hunger, or oppression, indicates that evil is relative. God does not decree cruelty. Says Kaplan, we should identify God with the sum of those organizing forces in the world which continue to bring order in the universe. Therefore, when evil strikes, we should not despair but trust and hope that one day it will be totally eliminated.

Kaplan recognized that this analysis does not represent a theoretical solution to the problem of evil.

> It is the only way in which the human being will ever learn to adjust himself to it creatively.
> (Ibid., p. 73)

A question can be raised here: To whom should we turn in order to seek help against evil? Humanity, writes Kaplan, must "act on faith in life's unlimited creative possibilities" (ibid., p. 81).

The world has not reached its finality but is continually being renewed by God and in need of improvement by all of us. In this area we have a responsibility, and that is to join as copartners with God in eliminating all evil from the universe.

In Summary

A great thinker of our time, Kaplan advanced a God concept which can be understood within the context of our own human experience. Rejecting God as a supernatural power, Kaplan argued that God is the totality of all those forces which help us become the best people are capable of becoming. He viewed prayer primarily as the ability to express one's own wishes and to provide an incentive for a program of action. He saw evil as that aspect of the universe which still needs to be conquered through cooperation with those creative forces that make human "salvation" possible.

10

THE HUMANISM OF FROMM

Background

Erich Fromm, one of the most respected humanists and social philosophers of the twentieth century, was born in Frankfurt, Germany, in 1900, into an Orthodox Jewish family. As a youngster, he received a good Jewish education which stressed the study of Bible and Talmud. In his teens, Fromm showed interest in social studies, philosophy, and psychology, and as a graduate student he attended the Psychoanalytic Institute of Berlin where he received his psychoanalytic training.

When Hitler rose to power in 1933, Fromm left Germany and moved to New York City and became a U.S. citizen. In 1949, due to his wife's poor health, he went to Mexico. In 1974, Fromm retired to Switzerland where he continued to work until his death in 1980.

During his lifetime, Fromm sought a rational solution to political problems. He was a pacifist and one of the organizers of the National Committee for a Sane Nuclear Policy.

One of his major concerns was how to deal with human isolation, feelings of insignificance, and doubt about the meaning of life. He observed that people were becoming alienated and indifferent to the feelings of others as a result of the rapid proliferation of technology. He, therefore, recommended a

return to a simpler life within the framework of a humanistic philosophy that he described in such works as *Psychoanalysis and Religion, The Art of Loving,* and *You Shall Be as Gods.*

Vital Human Needs

In a 1956 lecture at the Hebrew Union College-Jewish Institute of Religion in Cincinnati, Fromm identified the basic human needs as follows:

1. *Relatedness:* Every person needs to relate to the outside world. This could be accomplished by submitting to or by having power over someone else. But neither one is satisfactory. The best way to associate with others is through personal integrity and love.

2. *Rootedness:* Each one of us needs to have a sense of belonging. We need to be rooted, as Fromm expressed it, "in the brotherhood of man."

3. *Transcendence:* Human beings need to become creators.

Whenever the capacity for creation fails, the wish for destruction becomes the predominant pattern.
(*Man, the Family, the Social and Cultural System,*
ed. Robert L. Katz, p. 101; Cincinnati: HUC)

4. *Sense of identity:* We need to know who we are. If a member of a primitive tribe were to be asked, "Who are you?" he would answer, "I am we." That, however, is not enough.

I must be able to say "I." I must be able to experience myself as an "I." . . . Only if I am the true originator and creator of my own psychic acts, the true master of my own human powers, only then will I have the experience which permits me to have a sense of identity.

(Ibid.)

5. *Frame of orientation and devotion:* We must make some sense of our world. We need to have an integrated picture of reality.

Definition of Religion

According to Fromm, religion is a fundamental human need. In fact, he derives his definition of religion from the list of our basic personal necessities.

I understand by religion any system of thought and action shared by a group which gives the individual a frame of orientation and an object of devotion.
(*Psychoanalysis and Religion,* p. 21; Yale, 1959)

There is no individual, or culture, which does not have a religious need; that is, a frame of orientation and an object of devotion. We all look at the world from a particular vantage point and cherish certain high ideals. However, this tells us very little about the content of our needs. A person may worship animals, trees, idols, money, leaders. In fact:

> If we scratch the surface of modern man we discover any number of individualized primitive forms of religion.
>
> (Ibid., p. 29)

Therefore:

> The question is not religion or not but which kind of religion, whether it is one furthering man's development, the unfolding of his specifically human powers, or one paralyzing them.
>
> (Ibid. p. 26)

Two Types of Religion

Fromm distinguished between "authoritarian" and "humanistic" religions.

Authoritarian religions emphasize the idea that human beings are controlled by a higher power outside of themselves. Furthermore, they teach that this higher power is "entitled" to obedience, reverence, and worship.

> The essential element in authoritarian religion and in the authoritarian religious experience is the surrender to a power transcending man.
>
> (Ibid., p. 35)

The main virtue in an authoritarian religion is obedience; the greatest sin is disobedience. By submitting to the powerful authority of the deity, the individual escapes from his/her feeling of loneliness and limitation. God here is a symbol of power and force. Consequently:

The more perfect God becomes, the more imperfect becomes man. He projects the best he has onto God and thus impoverishes himself.

> (Ibid., p. 50)

On the other hand, humanistic religions are centered around human strengths. The goal here is to develop our power of reason in order to gain a better understanding of ourselves, our relations to others, our limitations and capabilities. The highest virtue in humanistic religion is not obedience, but self-realization. In the words of Fromm:

> [Faith is] certainty of conviction based on one's experience of thought and feeling, not assent to propositions on credit of the proposer.
>
> (Ibid., p. 37)

The person with an "authoritarian conscience" is a dutiful individual. The danger is, however, that this person may also carry out the orders of a superior regardless of their content. History records numerous crimes committed in the name of duty and conscience. On the other hand, a person with a "humanistic conscience" does not operate with the idea of pleasing or displeasing another. In essence:

> The humanistic conscience is the voice of our self which summons us back to ourselves, to become what we potentially are.
>
> (*You Shall Be as Gods,* p. 45; Fawcett Premier, 1969)

Here a question could be raised: If by espousing a humanistic religion we are urged to become the best of what we can be, does this mean that a "thief" should try to become the "best thief in town"? Obviously not! A human being, Fromm reminds us, must follow the good path and not the evil path.

For a humanist, anything that furthers life is "good"; anything that arrests or strangles it is "evil." Therefore, a thief must give up his "evil" profession and do productive work in society to become an ethical and religious person.

Most religions, including Judaism, have gone through an authoritarian stage, in which God appeared as a supreme Ruler commanding certain actions. Fromm's hope is that as religions develop they will recognize the values of "humanism" and move away from "authoritarianism."

However, this does not mean that we must give up our sense of belonging or deny our limitations and dependencies.

> It is one thing to recognize one's dependence and limitations, and it is something entirely different to indulge in this dependence, to worship the forces on which one depends. . . . The one is humility, the other self-humiliation.
>
> (*Psychoanalysis and Religion,* p. 53)

God: Symbol of Our Highest Powers

According to Fromm, God is not a power standing over us, telling us what to do or not to do from a lofty and distant position. Fromm maintains:

> [God] stands for the highest value, the most desirable good. Hence, the specific meaning of God depends on what is the most desirable good for a person.
>
> (*The Art of Loving,* p. 63; Harper & Bros., 1956)

For Fromm, this "most desirable good" is the ability to develop our own powers to the highest potential; in other words, to become the best of what we can be. God, in Fromm's opinion, represents the supreme goal for humanity.

The goal of finding union with the world through full development of his [the individual's] specifically human capacities of love and reason.

(You Shall Be, p. 21)

In Fromm's system, therefore, God is not a reality outside of humankind, or beyond the world, but an "idea," a symbol in our minds.

God is one of the many different poetic expressions of the highest value in humanism, not a reality in itself.

(Ibid., p. 18)

Yet, this does not mean that God is less real for every individual. God stands for a goal toward which each one of us must strive. In Fromm's words:

God is a symbol of man's own powers which he tries to realize in his life, and is not a symbol of force and domination, having power over man.

(Psychoanalysis and Religion, p. 37)

Simply stated:

God is the image of man's higher self, a symbol of what man potentially is or ought to become.

(Ibid., p. 49)

If we were to ask, "Is God outside of us, or inside of us?" Fromm would answer: God is only inside of us as an idea, an image, a symbol of what we can ultimately become.

Thus, in defining his concept of God, Fromm places himself among the non-theists. In fact, he has identified his position specifically as "non-theistic mysticism." This means that he does not believe that God is a spiritual reality transcending humankind. He also considers himself a mystic. Here is how he defines the ultimate religious experience:

> The experience of oneness with the All, based on one's relatedness to the world as it is grasped with thought and with love.
>
> (Ibid., p. 37)

Imitation of God

If God is only a value, a concept, an idea, and not a reality outside of us, how can we "know" God? Fromm taught that it is impossible for anyone to "know" God. According to Fromm, God actually stands for an inner human experience, and no concept can adequately express the totality of this experience. It may point to it, but it is not "it."

We human beings have an inherent tendency to strive for systematization and completeness. Yet, we must realize that we can obtain only "fragmentary" knowledge of God. Fromm points out that in Jewish tradition God is referred to as YHVH, with an underlying meaning of "becoming," and consequently there is very little to say about God. The only thing we can know is *"that* God is," not *"what* God is."

> Any talk about God—hence all theology—implies using God's name in vain. . . . Idols have names; they are things. They are not becoming—they are finished. Hence one can talk about them.
>
> (*You Shall Be,* p. 39)

The essence of Jewish religion, Fromm reminds us, is not "theology," which is "knowledge of God," but rather, "imitation of God." What we must do is to acquire and practice the main qualities that characterize God, primarily, justice and love.

> This imitation of God by acting the way God acts means becoming more and more like God; it means at the same time knowing God.
>
> (Ibid., p. 55)

The Rabbis of old had already taught something similar. Commenting on the biblical verse, "To walk in all His ways" (Deut. 11:22), they asked, "Which are God's ways?" They are as it is written, "The Lord, the Lord, God, merciful and gracious" (SJV/Exod. 34:6). Just as God is called merciful and gracious, so, the Rabbis added, you be merciful and gracious. (See *Sifre Deuteronomy, Ekev* 49.) Thus, though humans cannot *become* God in Judaism, they can be *like* God when they try to assimilate the highest human values attributed to God. Fromm writes:

> The truly religious person, if he follows the essence of the monotheistic idea, does not pray for anything, does not expect anything from God; he does not love God as a child loves his father or his mother; he has acquired the humility of sensing his limitations, to the degree of knowing that he knows nothing about God. God becomes to him a symbol in which man, at an earlier stage of his evolution, has expressed the totality of that which man is striving for, the realm of the spiritual world, or love, truth, and justice. He has faith in the principles which "God" represents; he thinks truth, lives love and justice. . . . To love God . . . would mean, then, to long for the attainment of full capacity to love, for the realization of that which "God" stands for in oneself.
>
> (*The Art of Loving*, p. 71)

Our goal in life, therefore, is to practice the values that God represents, mainly by speaking the truth, by dispensing justice, and by becoming loving individuals.

Religious Experience

Given Fromm's definition of religion and God, how does a religious experience or person differ from a non-religious experience or person? Fromm suggests the following points:

1. For a non-religious person, life is not a problem requiring a solution. Religious people, on the other hand, experience life as a question necessitating an answer. They do not take existence for granted. They display constant amazement and wonder at the world as they attempt to probe the question of how to relate to the universe around us.

2. In a religious experience, there is a hierarchy of values. The highest value in the list is the optimal development of one's moral and spiritual powers.

3. For a person having a religious experience, human beings are never used as a means, but always as an end in themselves.

4. A religious experience is one of letting go of one's ego, of one's greed, of one's fears.

> How can one see, hear, love, if one is filled with one's ego, if one is driven by greed?
>
> (*You Shall Be*, p. 49)

5. A religious experience is one in which a person can go beyond him/herself, by "leaving the prison of one's selfishness and separateness" (ibid., p. 49).

In other words, it is the elimination of self-love for the sake of relating to others with openness and a sense of generosity.

In Summary

Fromm based his understanding of God and religion on human needs. He recognized that every individual has a particular orientation to life and cherishes an object of devotion. This religious need, however, can bring people either to an authoritarian or to a humanistic approach to religion. Fromm urges that we move away from the first and espouse the second, based on his belief that we can find oneness with the world, not by regressing to the prehuman state, but by developing our specifically human qualities of love and reason. God, for Fromm, characterizes these ideas and stands for the highest human values which give meaning to our lives.

FINDING YOUR PLACE

Now that you have seen the ten different Jewish perspectives, you can perhaps better understand why we have come to question the statement, "I don't believe in God." When Jews say this, most of them really mean that they find it difficult to accept the biblical or rabbinic views of God.

Perhaps you are one of those individuals. And perhaps you also belong to that great majority of Jews who have never been exposed to the ideas of the Jewish thinkers we have selected, or to others who have had an equally significant impact on Jewish thought.

Whenever *we* encounter the statement, "I don't believe in God," we answer with a question, "What is it that you don't believe?" Whatever the response, we have the opportunity to introduce some of the information contained in this book. More often than not, those to whom we speak express surprise at finding a Jewish thinker whose God concept is "just like mine." This makes it possible for those Jews to "include themselves in" Judaism in a spiritual sense.

Before we ask you to attempt to place yourself in the Jewish theological spectrum, let's briefly review a number of logical conclusions that we can derive from our study:

1. *Numerous and varied God concepts are valid within Judaism.*
2. *Though classical theism may be the most common Jewish theological position, it is by no means the only one possible.* Atheism, therefore, is frequently not a rejection of God but rather a rejection of classical theism. A self-styled non-believer may be surprised to learn that he or she is really a Jewish religious naturalist, a Jewish humanist, a Jewish pantheist, or other.
3. *No single interpretation qualifies as "the" Jewish God concept.* Centuries ago, the compilers of the *siddur* apparently held this same belief, as the *Avot* prayer demonstrates:

> Blessed are You, O Lord Our God,
> God of Abraham, God of Isaac, and God of Jacob.

It would have been simpler just to write "God of Abraham, Isaac, and Jacob." But that is not how it reads. The word "God" is repeated *three* times:

> *God* of Abraham
> *God* of Isaac
> *God* of Jacob

Commenting on this seeming lack of economy in language, our Sages declared that this formulation was no accident. The author of this prayer, they asserted, was telling us that, though each of the patriarchs believed in one God, he experienced that God in different ways. On the other hand, not every God concept is compatible with Judaism. For example, any religion that considers a human being to be God, or as part of the Deity, remains outside of Judaism. In Judaism, human beings are considered "finite" and, there-fore, can never be worshiped as God.

If the patriarchs of Judaism could differ in their experience of God, then surely we, their descendants, have the same privilege.

4. *Our ideas of God can change.* Many of the Jewish philosophers whose teachings we have explained felt that theological answers, beyond those commonly accepted in their time, were required to respond satisfactorily to troublesome questions. We, today, are the beneficiaries of their study and reflection and are free, as well, to expand their spiritual horizons.

5. *We, individually, and Jews, as a whole, need to engage in more extensive study of Jewish options for belief.* Only through study can we become aware of our alternatives and thus obtain the tools with which we might determine our own place in the Jewish spiritual community.

These conclusions lead us at last to a confrontation and exploration of self. To begin the process, please set aside some quiet time and write out your *personal* responses to the following questions:

- What is God's nature?
- Is there only one God?
- How can I know God?
- How does God relate to the world?
- Does God have a special relationship with the Jewish people?
- What does God "want" from people?
- Can I have a personal relationship with God?
- How can I explain the presence of evil in the world?

In answering these questions, carefully and thoroughly, you have, in effect, set down your personal Jewish theology. Each of us is, in a very real sense, a Jewish philosopher, with something important to say to our peers, our friends, and our family.

A famous writer once remarked that friendship begins at

that moment when one person says to another, "You too? I thought I was the only one!" If that is true, then some of you are about to make a new friend.

The following chart represents a brief, comparative look at the thinkers we have examined. Read through it and note where your personal answers to the questions we posed are the same as—or close to—the ideas of a particular Jewish system. For example, if your theological profile affirms that God is nature, you may be closest to the teachings of Spinoza. Or, if you believe that God is limited, you may discover that you and Milton Steinberg are very similar in your ideas.

If there is *one* particular great thinker whose thoughts you share, you have achieved two ends. First, you have discovered a theological "friend." Second, you have placed yourself in the Jewish theological continuum.

You may find, however, that there are several thinkers, *part* of whose philosophy matches your own. In that case, we hope you will read and study further. The positions outlined in this book are not the only possible ones within Judaism. There are other alternatives which were not included because of the limitations of space and scope of this introductory volume. In pursuing your search, you may decide that there is a single theology with which you are most comfortable. Or, you may find that you have synthesized many theologies and created your own, unique, but within a Jewish context.

Whatever you determine, we will be happy knowing that a part of that process involved an examination of options and a choice based on knowledge rather than uncritical acceptance.

Finally, we hope that you will take it as your personal responsibility to share your knowledge with others, to urge them to study, to talk about God and belief without embarrassment. Exploring our relationship with God is not the exclusive province of theologians. It is the right, privilege, and responsibility of *every* Jew.

Appendix

	In the Bible	In Rabbinic Literature	Philo: Spiritual Monotheism	Maimonides: Neo-Aristotelianism	Luria: Mysticism
God's Nature	Different notions, some derived from other Near Eastern religions.	No systematic notion	God is the "Soul" of the universe, the universal "Mind," pure spirit or intelligence.	God is pure intellect, the Unmoved Mover of the universe.	God is En Sof, infinite, revealed to us through the ten sefirot. At the same time God is self-limited. Therefore, God needs us to "mend" the world.
Basic Questions	God exists. But is God among us? What is God's name? What does God want of us?	God exists. How can we serve God?	Does God exist? Does God have two parts, body and soul?	Does God exist? How should we interpret the attributes of God?	How can we ascend the ladder of creation and return to God?
God's Unity	An early notion that there may be gods for other nations gave way to a firm belief that there is only one God for all humanity. Angels exist, but only as God's messengers.	God is one, not two, and unique. Denied the existence of any other divine power in the universe. Angels exist, but only as God's messengers.	God is one. We can prove that God exists.	God is one. We can prove that God exists.	God is One.
God's Name	Proper name of YHVH, not to be pronounced. Other names used to describe powers of God or ways in which God relates to the world (El, Elohim, El Shaddai, Adon, Tzur, Av, Melech).	New names introduced: Hagevurah, Harachaman, Hamakom, Ribono shel olam, Avinu shebashamayim, and others.	God can only be called Ontos, a Greek term for "That which exists."	Whatever we call God is inadequate, for our language is limited.	En Sof (The Endless One).

	In the Bible	In Rabbinic Literature	Philo: Spiritual Monotheism	Maimonides: Neo-Aristotelianism	Luria: Mysticism
Knowing God	Some texts assert that a few people "saw" God or "met" God, but these texts provide no specific description.	We cannot know God.	We cannot describe God. God is unknowable.	God is incorporeal. We cannot say what God "is," only what God "is not."	God is totally unknowable by the human mind.
God's Relationship to the World	God alone created the world, established a predictable order for it, and continually renews it. God's might and concern for humanity are revealed through historical and natural events.	God judges the world. God rewards the good and punishes the wicked.	The "logos" is the means through which God operates in the world.	God created the world out of God's will, *ex nihilo* (out of nothing). God rules the world through "angels," divine intellects. God put in them the forces that govern and shape the physical world.	In observing the physical world, we derive the existence of *En Sof* as its cause.
God and the People Israel	God revealed the Torah at Sinai. God brought Israel into the Promised Land. God and Israel are in a covenantal relationship. Israel is to obey God's laws. God is to protect Israel as God's chosen people for all generations.	God gave Israel both a Written and an Oral Torah at Sinai. God "loves" the people Israel. Israel loves God. The relationship is an unbreakable one. God protects us and cares for us. God will resurrect the dead in the world-to-come.	Revelation is God's special gift to Israel. Israel receives the highest form of prophecy.	Israel is the chosen people. The Torah and the *mitzvot* help us realize our divine potential.	God and Israel are copartners. Through the performance of *mitzvot*, we free the imprisoned divine sparks and help to restore the world. Through prayer, our soul ascends to God.

What God "Wants"	God requires observance of *mitzvot* and ethical behavior.	God requires observance of *mitzvot* and ethical behavior.	Observing the biblical prescriptions is not enough. We must attempt to understand their spiritual essence.	God is distant from the world. We have free will to shape our world. But God "knows" the choices we will make in a manner that is beyond our comprehension.	God "wants" and "needs" us to better ourselves and restore the world.
God and the Individual	God is a personal God, who hears and answers prayer. God is compared to a parent who cares and watches lovingly over us. God is seen as having human qualities, such as anger, compassion, and a capacity for love.	God is a personal God, who hears and answers prayer. God has the capacity for compassion and anger, but God "prefers" mercy.	We can direct prayer to God, but that is merely our way of talking "about" God. Only through development of our reason can we approach God.	We can pray directly to God and draw nearer to God as our intellectual level increases. The highest goal in life is intellectual and spiritual perfection.	Meditation, prayer, and contemplation give us knowledge about God's relation to our world. People represent the Divine Presence on earth. We can commune with God.
The Problem of Evil	God is loving and just, yet there is evil in the world. Different notions: evil is punishment for sin, a test, beyond our comprehension. No single idea.	God is loving and just. Suffering may be a punishment for sin, but why the righteous suffer is beyond our comprehension. This world is not the only one. There is another world *ha-olam haba* (the world-to-come) when the righteous will be rewarded and the wicked punished.	Evil is a consequence of the imperfection of the physical world and, therefore, was not caused and cannot be remedied by God. Humanity is endowed with free will and, thus, must choose virtue. But humanity must choose virtue for its own sake as virtue leads to happiness.	Evil is the denial of good and has nothing to do with God. It is the result of the perishability of matter and the misuse of freedom by human beings.	Evil exists in the world as a result of *shevirat hakelim.* God needs us to eliminate evil.

	Spinoza: Pantheism	Buber: Dialogue	Steinberg: Limited Theism	Kaplan: Naturalism	Fromm: Humanism
God's Nature	God and the universe are one. God is nature. The laws of nature were set by God, and everything follows their structure.	God is the "Eternal Thou," always waiting for us to relate to God. God is an eternal presence that cannot be defined, described, or proven.	God is a Power and a Mind, the Being of all beings, purposive and ethical. But God is not all-powerful. God is like a parent who loves us but cannot save us from pain.	God is the totality of those forces in the world that render human life worthwhile. God is Power or "Process."	God is a symbol, an idea, of our highest potential, the most desirable good.
Basic Questions	What is God? How can we know God?	How can we open ourselves to genuine "I-Thou" encounter?	How do we reconcile the notion of God with the problem of evil and free will?	How can we attain self-realization?	How can the idea of God lead us to better ourselves?
God's Unity	God is One. There is no dualism of mind and matter.	God cannot be defined in any way. God can only be "met."	God is One.	God is One, in the sense of being a totality of forces leading to human self-realization.	God is a unique idea, a symbol in our minds, but not a reality in itself. God represents the supreme goal for humanity.
God's Name	No unique name.	The "Eternal Thou."	No unique name.	"The Power that makes for salvation."	No unique name. Any name for God makes God an idol.

Knowing God	God is the totality of the universe. The more we know about the structure of the world, the more we know about God.	One can meet God through a genuine dialogue with others.	We cannot know God completely. Our human knowledge is inadequate. We must accept the existence of God on faith. Logic alone cannot bring us to belief.	The human mind cannot know the totality of God. God is a power and thus has no appearance.	Imitating God means knowing God.
God's Relationship to the World	The laws of nature are manifestations of God. God does not act independently of the world. God is the world.	God waits everywhere in the world for us to let God in through a genuine dialogue.	God has a relationship with the world and needs humankind's help to improve it.	The world has not reached its finality but is continually being renewed by God.	God has no relationship to the world as such. Our idea of God places God in the world.
God and the People Israel	God has no special relationship to Israel or to any other people. The laws of nature, God, operate equally for all.	Sinai was not a one-time revelation of laws for all time. Revelation is possible at any time.	No particular notion.	Tradition has permanent values that we cannot afford to ignore.	God has no special relationship to any people. But the idea of God should inspire all people.
What God "Wants"	God "wants" nothing. God as nature simply "is."	God "wants" genuine encounter with humankind.	God needs and wants us to work for a more decent world.	Our prayers are for ourselves, not directed to some supernatural being. God is not supernatural, and thus does not "want" anything.	Our idea of God should move us to self-betterment, greater justice, and love. We thus should strive to "imitate" God.

	Spinoza: Pantheism	Buber: Dialogue	Steinberg: Limited Theism	Kaplan: Naturalism	Fromm: Humanism
God and the Individual	God is not a personal God. God is the laws of nature. The world is determined. Our only freedom comes through knowledge.	Whenever we have an "I-Thou" relationship with another person, we also encounter God, the "Eternal Thou." We receive a revelation of God's presence.	God allows us free will so that we can work together with God.	A God who makes a difference in one's personal life should be designated as a personal God.	God has no "relationship" with people outside of our idea of God. God is an inner human experience. We cannot know God.
The Problem of Evil	Good and evil are relative to human experience and have nothing to do with God.	Evil is the predominance of relating to others in an "I-It" fashion. Evil can be transcended through an "I-Thou" encounter. God's face is hidden before "radical evil."	Evil is part of the lower levels of evolutionary development. God cannot be blamed for evil and tragedy. Evil is part of the make-up of the universe and part of nature that has not yet been conquered.	Evil is that part of the universe that God has not yet subdued. The world has not reached its finality and our responsibility as copartners with God is to eliminate all evil from the universe.	Whatever hinders good is evil. Since God is an image of our higher selves God has nothing to do with evil in the world. It is therefore the task of people to eliminate evil through greater truth, goodness, and kindness.

Bibliography

(This bibliography includes studies quoted in this book.)

Bible

Gates of Prayer: The New Union Prayer Book. New York: Central Conference of American Rabbis, 1975.

The New Oxford Annotated Bible, Revised Standard Version. New York: Oxford University Press, 1973.

A New Translation of the Holy Scriptures: The Torah (1962), *The Prophets* (1978), and *The Writings* (1982). Philadelphia: Jewish Publication Society of America (JPS).

Rabbinic Literature

Mekilta de Rabbi Ishmael, trans. J.Z. Lauterbach. 3 vols. Philadelphia: JPS, 1933.

Midrash Rabbah, ed. H. Freedman and M. Simon. 10 vols. 3rd ed. London and New York: Soncino, 1983.

A Rabbinic Anthology, C.G. Montefiore and H. Loewe. Cleveland and New York: The World Publishing Company, Meridian Books, 1963.

Seder Eliahu Rabba, M. Friedmann. Jerusalem: Bamberger, 1960.

The Soncino Talmud. 18 vols. London and New York: Soncino, 1935.

Philo

Loeb Classical Library. Colson and Whitaker edition, 1961.

Maimonides

The Guide to the Perplexed, trans. Shlomo Pines. Chicago: University of Chicago, 1963.

A Maimonides Reader, Isadore Twersky. New York: Behrman House, 1972.

Luria

Back to the Sources, ed. Barry W. Holtz. New York: Summit Books, 1984.
The Zohar, trans. H. Sperling and M. Simon. 5 vols. London: Soncino, 1956.

Spinoza

Chief Works of Benedict de Spinoza, trans. R.H.M. Elwes. London: Bell, 1884.

Buber

Between Man and Man, trans. R.G. Smith. New York: Macmillan, 1965.
I and Thou, trans. R.G. Smith. 2nd ed. New York: Scribner's, 1958.
On Judaism, ed. Nahum N. Glatzer. New York: Schocken, 1972.
On the Bible, ed. Nahum N. Glatzer. New York: Schocken, 1968.

Steinberg

Anatomy of Faith. New York: Harcourt, Brace and World Inc., 1960.
A Believing Jew. New York: Harcourt, Brace and World Inc., 1951.
Basic Judaism. New York: Harcourt, Brace and World Inc., 1947.

Kaplan

Judaism without Supernaturalism. New York: Jewish Reconstructionist Press, 1958.
The Meaning of God in Modern Jewish Religion. New York: Jewish Reconstructionist Press, 1962.
Questions Jews Ask. New York: Jewish Reconstructionist Press, 1956.

Fromm

The Art of Loving. New York: Harper and Bros., 1956.
Psychoanalysis and Religion. New Haven: Yale University, 1959.
You Shall Be as Gods. New York: Fawcett Premier, 1969.

About the Authors

Rifat Sonsino is the rabbi of Temple Beth Shalom in Needham, Massachusetts. A graduate of HUC-JIR, he holds a Ph.D. from the University of Pennsylvania.

Daniel B. Syme, a rabbi and graduate of HUC-JIR, holds a doctorate in education from Teachers College, Columbia University. For ten years, he served as director of the UAHC-CCAR Commission on Jewish Education and is now a vice-president of the Union of American Hebrew Congregations.